Work in the Fast Lane

SUNY Series,
THE NEW INEQUALITIES

Anthony Gary Dworkin, Editor

Work in the Fast Lane

Flexibility, Divisions of Labor, and Inequality in High-Tech Industries

Glenna Colclough
and
Charles M. Tolbert II

STATE UNIVERSITY OF NEW YORK PRESS

Published by
State University of New York Press, Albany

For information, address State University of New York
Press, State University Plaza, Albany, N.Y. 12246

Production by Ruth Fisher
Marketing by Bernadette LaManna

Library of Congress Cataloging-in-Publication Data

Colclough, Glenna, 1951–
    Work in the fast lane : flexibility, divisions of labor, and
    inequality in high-tech industries / Glenna Colclough and Charles M.
    Tolbert II.
        p.   cm. — (SUNY series, the new inequalities)
    Includes index.
    ISBN 0–7914-0783–7 (alk. paper) . — ISBN 0–7914-0784–5 (pbk.
alk. paper)
        1. High technology industries—Management. 2. High technology
industries—Personnel management. 3. High technology industries—
Employees. 4. Division of labor. I. Tolbert, Charles M.
II. Title. III. Series: SUNY series in the new inequalities.
HD62.37.C65   1992
331.25—dc20
                                                        90–20851
                                                        CIP

10 9 8 7 6 5 4 3 2 1

For our teachers,

Woody Beck and Pat Horan

Contents

List of Figures

List of Tables

Acknowledgments

Several friends and colleagues helped us bring this project to fruition. Rick Christenson and Walter Sullins assisted with computer programming. John Tichenor made many trips to the library and spent hours going over early drafts. In conjunction with his thesis research, Joe Parks assisted in developing the 21-year CPS data series. Wanda Mitchell cheerfully and most competently managed word processing throughout the project. We also thank the anonymous reviewers for their careful and supportive commentary. Finally, we are especially grateful to Gary Dworkin, SUNY Series Editor, for his initial enthusiasm for the research and for his subsequent encouragement.

This research contributes to U.S.D.A. Regional Project S–229 in which we both participate as technical committee members. A major data resource for this monograph is Public Use Microdata Sample D, 1980 U.S. Census, which was developed with the assistance of the Agriculture and Rural Economy Division, Economic Research Service, U.S.D.A. Our collaboration has also been facilitated by a research development grant from the Florida State University Council for Research and Creativity. Of course, none of these supportive individuals and institutions necessarily endorses our conclusions.

We are grateful nonetheless.

Chapter One

Introduction

The transition is incomplete. Once the most powerful industrial nation, the United States is in the midst of a difficult transition from a manufacturing to a service economy. Key traditional industries that sustained America's middle class throughout the twentieth century are in decline. Skilled blue-collar jobs in steel, rubber, and automotive industries that provide good pay and benefits plus opportunities for upward mobility are dwindling. The new service sector is sharply divided between high-skill professional pursuits and low-skill service occupations; between software designers on the one hand and people grilling hamburgers on the other. While the standards of living for the upper and working classes continue to diverge, middle-class lifestyles are increasingly confined to dual-earner families. Amid this transformation to a new industrial order, the public optimism of the postwar years has been replaced with caution, doubt, and uncertainty. In this changing context, it is important that researchers chart and understand emerging forms of social stratification.

The increasing economic polarization of the U.S. population has been well documented by economists and sociologists.[1] Poverty rates in the 1980s have increased across the country. The middle class has been described as "shrinking." A recent wave of corporate mergers in the wake of industrial deregulation suggests that wealth is becoming more concentrated. The optimistic prognostications of postindustrialists like Daniel Bell about job and skill upgrading continue to be challenged by researchers in the tradition of Harry Braverman who focus on deskilling and degradation of work.[2] To understand the increasing gap between the affluent and the plebeian that characterizes the 1980s, sociologists and economists alike are turning to structural theories that look beyond the characteristics of individuals. Popular in an

1

age of economic growth and affluence, individualistic theories of income determination and aggregate income inequality have given way to perspectives that can account for individual failures despite high skill levels, high motivation, and extensive work experience. The characteristics of individuals—their human capital and social distinctions—are increasingly understood to operate within a complex and variable mosaic of industrial, market, occupational, and organizational contexts.

One piece of this mosaic and its consequences for economic inequality are the foci of this book. High technology is a single industrial sector that employs at best 10 percent of the U.S. labor force. Nonetheless, high-tech industries are for the most part expanding rapidly as we approach the end of the century. More importantly, high technology is an industrial sector that many hope will be the basis for a new national economy that elevates the United States back to its former dominance in the international marketplace. A sector on which so many hopes are pinned deserves close scrutiny.

High technology's work structures—industrial, occupational, and organizational—have important implications not only for workers in that sector, but for those in other sectors of the economy linked to particular high-tech industries. What do these work structures portend for stratification and inequality inside high-tech industries as well as outside the sector? We begin to answer this question by attempting to clarify what we mean by high-tech industries. As it turns out, in developing a definition for this sector it is necessary to raise several issues.

HIGH TECHNOLOGY: DEFINITIONAL ISSUES[3]

Though there is much discussion of high tech in the media, the term has diverse meanings. There is a conventional definition of high technology used by a number of labor-force researchers that we opt to use for reasons outlined below. Still, there are a number of issues that we considered in settling on this definition. One difficulty in defining high technology is that the term is relative to time and place. Industrial capitalism is dynamic, and development within it is frequently uneven. This means that what is considered high tech at one point in time or in one place may not be considered high tech at some other time or place. In the South, the use of electronic knitting machines, electronically controlled looms, and robots in the textile industry is considered high-tech production.[4] Yet these techniques are deemed quite commonplace in regions where textile manufacturing has advanced more rapidly.

A second definitional problem is the considerable confusion in the literature over the appropriate unit of analysis. Is high tech embodied in a job, an occupation, an industry, or a firm? The most common unit of analysis used by researchers is that of industry. Industry is attractive because of the standard industry coding schemes available on data files for firms and individuals. Moreover, industries can be grouped into an intuitively appealing high-tech sector that can be contrasted with other industrial sectors. Drawbacks include the fact that a broadly defined industrial category may include the production of both technologically sophisticated products and rather simple things. Telephones and satellites, for instance, are both included under the communications equipment industry category which is treated as a high-tech industry in most schemes.

While an industry's products may be technologically complex, the process by which they are produced may be very simple and involve little skill. Boards for personal computers are very sophisticated technological items, but their production is highly routinized and standardized. The most skilled production task is soldering certain components onto the board. Yet, this task is increasingly being done by machines. Workers involved in the production of computer boards operate machines, tend equipment, and manually clip wires off of individual components. The important issue here is whether high technology refers to *products* or *processes* by which products are made. That is, should the high-tech label be reserved for cutting-edge industries with large research and development components? Or, should high technology also encompass the use of standardized production processes to manufacture technologically sophisticated products? This is a distinction that some previous researchers have not maintained.[5]

A related issue is whether high-tech industry classifications should include only manufacturing industries or be broadened to encompass certain technologically sophisticated service industries such as computer software. These different approaches are exemplified on the one hand by the commonly employed Bureau of Labor Statistics definition which is limited to manufacturing industries.[6] On the other hand, a definitional scheme suggested by Edward Malecki includes both high-tech manufacturing and services.[7] The inclusion of services seems warranted, given the increasing importance of this sector in national and global economies. High-tech service industries provide employment in some of the fastest growing high-tech occupations and facilitate production in other industrial sectors.

Alternative units of analysis such as firms and occupations also present problems. Firms in which high-tech production takes place tend to be diversified; some products may be technologically complex and others may not. More pragmatically, data on firms are hard to find, and high-tech firms are particularly notorious for resisting data collection on their operations.[8] Occupation as an indicator of high tech is problematic because occupational categories do not necessarily take into account organizational and industrial contexts. Surely the computer programmer working on the Strategic Defense Initiative is more plausibly characterized as a high-tech worker than a temporary programmer configuring a database system for a law office. From an analytic standpoint, it is important to consider occupational distributions as consequences of particular types of high-tech industrial development. This precludes using occupation as the sole defining characteristic of high technology for certain research questions, including some we pose in this book.

A third type of definitional issue involves the different conceptions of high technology employed by various constituencies. The goals and concerns of academicians, industrial developers, and policymakers may be quite different, and a single definition may not suit the purposes of these different factions. Industrial development boards and chambers of commerce tend to employ very broad definitions of high technology, disregarding definitional problems associated with products, production processes, and units of analysis. Researchers frequently disagree with policymakers on what constitutes high-tech industries. Malecki, for example, contends that developers need to limit their definitions to only those truly innovative industries on the cutting edge of technology.[9] He notes that attracting high-tech manufacturing firms that employ standardized production techniques may run contrary to most policymakers' high-tech development goals. Instead of building an enclave of well-paid engineers and technicians, local officials may find themselves with a low-wage, high-tech equivalent of a textile mill.

Despite these definitional problems, we must at some point simply decide on a definition that is most useful in view of theoretical and practical considerations. The high-technology definition used throughout this book follows closely the Bureau of Labor Statistics' definition and is industry-based (i.e., product versus process oriented).[10] Following Malecki, however, the definition includes both service and manufacturing industries.[11] This results in a broad industrial scheme that encompasses industries that most developers and policymakers consider high technology. In the final analysis, it is these practitioners who are attempting to create high-tech communities across the nation and who may well shape the development of a high-tech economy for the twenty-first century.

As suggested by Malecki, our definition includes the following industries which can be readily identified on the census data files we employ:

> *Manufacturing:* Guided missiles and spacecraft, radio and TV receiving equipment, communications equipment, electronic components, aircraft and parts, office and computing machines, ordnance and accessories, drugs and medicines, industrial inorganic chemicals, professional and scientific instruments, engines and turbines, plastic material and synthetics.

> *Service:* Computer programming, data-processing, and other services; research and development laboratories; and management consulting.

With a working definition of high technology in hand, we now briefly introduce some of the promise and potential problems of high-tech industries that will be developed throughout the remainder of the book.

HIGH TECHNOLOGY: THE PROMISE

The importance of advanced technology for economic growth and progress has been expounded by social thinkers representing diverse theoretical orientations. Mainstream theorists like Bell and Lenski argue that technology brings progress and that the industrialization it fosters will ultimately lessen economic inequalities.[12] Radical theorists like Smith and Mandel see technology as an instrument of capital used to overcome crises in capitalist development and provide a basis for the expansion and ultimate survival of a capitalist economy.[13] Inequalities resulting from the uneven expansion of capital are seen as permanent and endemic features of capitalism.

Policymakers and regional and local industrial developers view technological progress as fundamental to economic growth and the survival of the American economy. The rapid growth in high-tech industries and enterprises that has occurred with particular intensity over the last two decades is a major manifestation of this philosophy. Fueled by a seemingly permanent war economy, the development of space- and defense-related industries has burgeoned in the postwar era. A quiet mill town of 25,000 people—Huntsville, Alabama—has been quickly transformed into a high-tech center of 200,000 inhabitants, many of whom work directly or indirectly for defense and other government contractors. The computer revolution has produced Silicon Valley and the Route 128 area near prestigious research universities like Stanford and MIT. Similarly, petrochemical processing has spawned community growth all along the Gulf Coast. In the Midwest, firms producing aircraft, engines, and electronic equipment are thriving in the midst of a regional employment tailspin.

In the wake of declining key industries like steel, aluminum, rubber, and automobiles, high-tech industries promise new jobs, higher wages, and growing markets to secure the U.S. economy of the twenty-first century. As intense interarea competition for business and economic growth continues, the high-tech mystique has inspired the imaginations of developers in large and small communities in metropolitan and nonmetropolitan areas alike. The U.S. economy is undergoing a dramatic transformation of its industrial base, and high-technology industries are viewed as important in facilitating this transition and in establishing a new economic regime.

HIGH TECHNOLOGY: POTENTIAL PROBLEMS

While many tout the promise of high-tech industrial development, others have argued for a critical assessment of its implications.[14] First, the reality of some high-tech work is that it entails very menial and tedious manual labor. Not all production is on the cutting edge, nor are all products produced with sophisticated production processes. Some high-tech work is no more glamorous than work in a textile mill. Second, high-tech industries are often characterized by a two-tier occupational structure. Managers, engineers, researchers, and technical personnel occupy the higher skill and wage levels while low-skill, low-wage production workers fill the lower occupational tier. These workers have very different work experiences and are controlled by very different managerial strategies.

Third, the nature of the high-tech sector and the organization of work in its lower tier make production jobs vulnerable and unstable. Capital mobility and automation are constant threats, and job security is a major problem for high-tech workers. Firms that find cheaper overseas labor more profitable may have little commitment to U.S. localities. Uncertainty can prevail in the upper tier of high-tech industries as well. In an era that is witnessing profound political and economic change in Eastern Europe, U.S. engineering and technical positions funded by defense and other government contracts are vulnerable to cutbacks.

A final reason to conduct a critical assessment of high-tech industrial development is that not all areas are attractive to high-tech industries. The stringent demands of high-tech employers cannot be met by many communities, and this results in an uneven development process within the sector and between high-tech and other industries. As we will detail below, these demands can include proximity to air transportation, related firms, and suppliers for increasingly prevalent just-in-time production processes that do not require large inventories on hand, but in the vicinity.

It is our view that distinctive patterns of stratification and inequality result from uneven development of high-tech industries, two-tier occupational configurations, and differences in types of workers recruited for various jobs within the high-tech sector. Moreover, the economic polarization of the U.S. economy may be exacerbated by the inequality patterns that prevail in high-tech industries. With high-tech industries increasingly sought to provide a foundation for economic restructuring, it is important to compare and contrast high-tech stratification patterns and organization of work with that of other industrial sectors.

In this book, we demonstrate both the promise and potential problems of high technology. We examine various divisions of labor that exist within this industrial sector and demonstrate the varied economic experiences of high-tech workers. We also illustrate the diversity of industries, occupations, labor markets, and labor forces that exists within the high-tech sector. We examine the economic consequences of high-tech industrialization for inequalities within and between high-tech areas in different regions of the country. The consequences of working in high-tech industries for racial and ethnic groups and women are of particular interest. Through these analyses, we hope to depict the current state of work in high-tech industries.

PLAN OF THE BOOK

Our theoretical framework links three major concepts for the study of high-tech industries and employment. These concepts are: flexibility, divisions of labor, and inequality. The first, flexibility, pertains to the organization of production in high-tech firms and their efforts to survive and succeed in this environment. High-tech employers perceive intense demands for flexibility from product markets, the nature of high-tech products, and the social and political environments in which the firms operate. Flexibility in the face of rapidly changing technologies and markets is thought to be the key to survival and prosperity. There are several ways in which flexibility is built into management strategies for high-tech firms, and each has its own consequences for the ways in which labor is organized, i.e., who does it, how it is done, and where it is done.

These issues form the basis of the second important concept for this study: divisions of labor. The concept of divisions of labor is important throughout our analyses of high-tech industries because these divisions are fundamental for understanding socioeconomic inequality among workers. While we typically think of the division of labor in *technical* terms—i.e., occupationally differentiated tasks that are necessary for the production of goods and services—there are other divisions of labor that are important as well. Marxist theory emphasizes *social* divisions of labor that involve possession of differential amounts of power, authority, and control. Similarly, labor segmentation theorists have noted the divisions within labor markets along racial, ethnic, and gender lines. Economic geographers have been very active in identifying the *spatial* division of labor that distributes work across locales within and between different industries and sectors.

These divisions of labor form a basis for inequalities in the determination of wages and the extraction of surplus value from the labor process. Moreover, the particular configurations of these divisions of labor are not the same for all sectors of the economy. In our analyses we demonstrate that the high-tech sector exhibits both traditional and distinctive divisions of labor which affect the socioeconomic outcomes of high-tech workers in several ways.

The final concept, inequality, is in part the result of the strategies for flexibility and resulting divisions of labor in high-tech work. We show that the patterns of inequality produced in the high-tech sector reflect and exacerbate trends in inequality among U.S. workers as a whole. In this way, the study of high-tech industries can provide a glimpse of the larger issues of inequality that are emerging in the economic transformation of American society. Through the application of these conceptual tools, we provide such a depiction in the chapters that follow.

The second chapter discusses the nature of flexibility sought by high-tech firms, alternative strategies for attaining flexibility, and their implications for the resulting divisions of labor. We focus on two types of flexibility: static and dynamic. Our review of research on work organization in high technology leads us to conclude that high-tech industries in the United States tend to borrow managerial strategies from more traditional industrial sectors. Even in the presumably progressive high-tech sector, these strategies result in the type of flexibility we characterize here as static. However, we note the potential for high-tech firms in the United States to employ more dynamic strategies, as have some of their international competitors.

The third chapter is the setting for an analysis of the labor force consequences of the emergence of the high-tech sector and accompanying strategies for flexible production. Using national samples of workers from 1970 through 1987, we trace the development of both technical and social divisions of labor in the high-tech sector and compare them to divisions of labor in other sectors. We explore variations in divisions of labor within the high-tech sector that are associated with different strategies for flexibility. Special attention is given to the distinctive intersection of the technical and social divisions of labor in high-tech industries. We shall see that labor is divided in such a way that minority labor force participants negatively experience the brunt of measures designed to make production more flexible, particularly when static flexibility is the managerial strategy.

High-tech development and the resulting spatial division of labor within the high-tech sector are examined in the fourth chapter. National, regional, and local high-tech industrialization policies are discussed. Theoretical perspectives that link the flexibility strategies of individual firms are reviewed as well. Then, through an analysis of census data, we identify high-tech centers in regions throughout the United States. Regional and local patterns of industrial and occupational mix are ascertained, and high-tech workers in these technology centers are compared to workers in other local industries. We report considerable heterogeneity among high-tech industries in the spatial distribution of employment opportunities.

In the fifth chapter, we continue the empirical study of high-tech workers as a national labor force and in different locales. We examine the socioeconomic implications of high-tech work and contrast it to other industries through analyses of earnings and earnings inequality. Regional comparisons of workers in high-tech centers are followed by comparisons of workers located in labor markets that do not have a large high-tech industry presence. The economic effects of local labor market contexts and different types of local economies on high-tech workers and their non-high-tech counterparts are assessed. Perhaps our most striking finding is that earnings inequality due to race, gender, and ethnicity is greater in the high-tech sector than in other industries. This holds for the national labor force as well as within local labor market settings.

In the final chapter of the book we summarize our research on the contemporary U.S. high-tech sector and then sketch some future scenarios for high-tech industries. This sector of the contemporary national economy could have important implications for the economy of the next century. Decisions about future courses of high-tech sector development ought to be made with full knowledge of implications for the economy and the social organization of work.

Chapter Two

The Nature and Organization of High-Tech Industries and Firms

Sterile-clad workers peering through microscopes in microelectronic assembly rooms contrast sharply with workers in a hot steel mill laboring against a backdrop of rusting smokestacks. Most of the electronic assembly is likely to be done by women. Men are likely to comprise the majority of workers in steel mills. While high-tech workers are not likely to be unionized, there is a strong tradition of collective bargaining among steel workers. Most importantly, the high-tech workers are associated with sunrise industries, and there is much reason for optimism about the growth potential of these industries. The steel industry, on the other hand, is thought to be in decline and has become something of a cash cow from which resources are diverted for more profitable ventures.

This contrast is indicative of a vast economic restructuring in which high-tech industries are seen by many as a crucial component in the emergent economies of the twenty-first century. To anticipate their role in the newly developing economies of the future, it is appropriate to review what we know about these industries—their organization, employment, and earnings patterns. This chapter will introduce the exemplars of high-tech success that have inspired local, regional, and national policymakers to exhort high-tech development. It is important to look beyond the rhetoric to understand the implications of these development models for jobs and people. As we shall see, while high-tech industries may share some characteristics with traditional industries, they have an uncommon need for flexibility. While strategies for flexible production have become more common in traditional industrial sectors, flexible production in the high-tech sector is business as usual. Flexibility is essential to high-tech indus-

11

tries that are on the cutting edge of innovation. Rapid technological developments and unstable markets demand a flexibility on the part of high-tech industries that shapes the kinds of jobs available, the number of jobs, and the rewards associated with them. In the sections that follow, we will discuss distinctive aspects of high-tech industries and the ways in which flexible structures and processes are implemented in this sector. We will also discuss several other modes of flexibility and the implications of these alternatives for the divisions of labor and the distribution of earnings within the high-tech sector.

HIGH-TECH EXEMPLARS: SILICON VALLEY AND ROUTE 128

The fervor for high-tech development began with the highly visible success of the first major high-tech center in California now known as Silicon Valley. This location became the core of the semiconductor industry, a collection of firms whose innovations have had a global impact.

Annalee Saxenian describes the transformation of a 1940s bucolic, agricultural Santa Clara County into a high-tech, industrial boomtown.[1] The preconditions of the area for its subsequent high-tech growth included established defense-related manufacturing industries (tanks, aircraft, and missiles), Moffet Field Naval Air Station, and the electrical engineering programs at Stanford University. Named for the inventor of the transistor, the first firm of the semiconductor industry, Shockley Transistor Company, found Santa Clara County a very inviting locale. This pioneering high-tech firm was a spinoff from Bell Laboratories in New Jersey. Over the next fifteen years after Shockley's entry into this new market in 1955, over 50 new spinoff firms were established. By the early 1970s, the name "Silicon Valley" was synonymous with the world capital of the semiconductor industry.

Saxenian details tremendous growth in population, rising income levels, and the upgrading of occupational structure that accompanied this industrial transformation in Silicon Valley. She also recognizes the boomtown problems that typify such rapid growth: inflated housing prices, traffic congestion, pollution, and the like. The unskilled and semiskilled production workers employed by these rapidly growing industries seemed to endure a disproportionate share of the boomtown problems. Forced by housing costs to live far from the plants, these workers found it necessary to commute long distances through congested traffic. The problems associated with Silicon Valley's uneven development process were ultimately addressed with a no-growth policy that severely restricted the location of new firms. Despite the need to locate production close to design in such rapidly changing industries, dispersion of the largest semiconductor and electronics manufacturing companies was also encouraged as the valley rapidly reached its limits in accommodating the economic, political, and social needs of its growing citizenry.[2]

Santa Clara was not the only stagnant local economy transformed by high technology. In the 1970s, the declining mill-based economy of New England experienced an economic renaissance of sorts with the growth of high-tech industries, particularly along Route 128 north of Boston. Bennett Harrison reports that from 1976 to 1978, the region experienced over 30 percent growth in employment. The leading sectors were high-tech industries such as instruments, computer manufacturing, and programming services.[3] Highly regarded computer firms such as Digital, Data General, Wang, and Prime located their headquarters in the region. Other firms, most notably IBM and Honeywell, maintained major production facilities there as well. One attraction for high-tech firms was the proximity to MIT and the business service sector of Boston. An equally important feature of the area was a compliant labor force experiencing high levels of unemployment.

Like Silicon Valley, the New England transformation was not without problems, nor were the advantages of economic growth enjoyed by all. Harrison argues that while new jobs were provided, real wages relative to other regions fell. Barriers to mobility existed in that indigenous workers in low-skill production jobs rarely had access to promotional ladders. Occupants of high-skill technical and professional positions were often recruited from outside the region. Like Silicon Valley, a polarization of income and quality of life was a product of the economic restructuring of the Route 128 corridor. The costs and benefits of the high-tech development process fell unevenly upon the region's inhabitants.

Those seeking to revitalize their local economic bases across the country have used these singular high-tech exemplars as models for development elsewhere. Yet, the Silicon Valley and New England case histories suggest positive and negative implications of a large high-tech presence in a local economy. Like any development in capitalist systems, the process is uneven in that all areas and people do not experience identical consequences of economic growth. This unevenness will become a theme of this monograph; i.e., employment experiences in high-tech industries are not uniform. Indeed, there may be less uniformity in the effects of employment in high-tech industries than in conventional industries due to their more polarized occupational structures, unique spatial requirements, and enhanced need for flexibility. The unevenness manifests itself in spatial, technical, and social divisions of labor that constitute bases for new forms of stratification and inequality.

Divisions of Labor

Spatial differentiation occurs as certain areas, due to natural, social, economic, and/or political characteristics, are more attractive to particular industries. As the U.S. economy enters into a more competitive phase in global markets and as our industrial base is restructured, new spatial patterns of firm location and expansion are emerging. High technology is an integral part of this restructuring process and has its own unique spatial patterns that have consequences for local economies, labor markets, opportunity structures, and qualities of life experienced by residents.

The *technical division of labor* is also contingent upon industrial structure and social relations of production in which corporate leaders decide how and where the production process will be organized. Within particular industries, production technologies, automation, and skill levels are tailored to unique products, markets, and ultimately, managerial prerogatives. High-tech industries are developing patterns of job and work organizations that are similar in some respects to other industrial sectors and are quite different in other ways.

Finally, the *social division of labor* consists of the segmentation of the labor force along racial, gender, and ethnic lines. In the traditional industrial order, employers' manipulation of these divisions within the working class has been an important strategy for reducing labor costs and inhibiting the development of class consciousness. By reserving the lowest skilled jobs for the least powerful workers (minorities), profits are enhanced and possibilities for overt labor-management conflict may be reduced—in the short run. High-tech industries, as we shall see, are no exception.

These divisions of labor and the consequences for workers and local labor markets will be major foci throughout this book. To understand the distinctive aspects of the divisions of labor in high-tech industries, we must first identify market characteristics that are particular to this sector. We argue that high degrees of uncertainty and greater needs for flexibility are features endemic to high-tech industries. Second, we discuss approaches to production flexibility that are likely to characterize high-tech industries. Finally, we consider the implications of flexible production strategies for these divisions of labor and the resulting stratification and inequality among workers.

HIGH TECH AS A RISKY BUSINESS

By definition, high-tech industries are innovative. Product lines and/or production techniques change constantly. Markets tend to be highly competitive structures in which small companies, as well as large ones, have opportunities for success. As evidenced by the forerunner of the Apple computer that Steve Jobs and Steve Wozniak fashioned in a garage, entry costs are relatively low in some high-tech industries because limited venture capital resources are required. A talented programmer with his or her own personal computer can develop software for a variety of computers and create a successful business in his or her own home. Examples of such efforts are abundant and occur in a wide variety of settings, including one-person firms and the wealthiest corporations in the world.

Innovations in Small and Large Firms

Innovation has been traditionally attributed to large firms because greater financial resources and economies of scale permit substantial incentives for innovation and a corporate emphasis on research and development. Recent critics of this hypothesis, however, argue that small firms actually hold an advantage for engaging in innovation. Large firms, by contrast, have relatively large amounts of capital invested in machinery which may be difficult to modify to meet new demands. Also, the organization of large firms is more likely to be bureaucratic, hence, inhibiting creativity and risk-taking. Smaller firms have less capital invested in older technologies and can offer greater incentives to innovative employees.

    An argument along these lines is outlined by marketing consultant Regis McKenna in his recent book, *Who's Afraid of Big Blue? How Companies are Challenging IBM and Winning*. In an interview reported in the *Huntsville Times*, McKenna argues that the proliferation of computing equipment and low-cost microprocessors has made the computer market widely accessible to new, small, and inventive businesses.[4] While IBM has maintained its dominance in the mainframe market, other companies like Tandy, Digital, and Apple have developed their own market niches in transaction processing, minicomputers, and school computers. IBM is burdened with a huge overhead, an unwieldy bureaucracy, and a traditional marketing strategy built on the mainframe market. According to McKenna, a rapidly expanding and fragmenting market structure and increasing demands for specialization and personalized service from new retail customers make it quite difficult for IBM to compete in many of the new computer-related markets.

A study by Nancy Dorfman on the relationships of firm size, market structures, and innovation concludes that different high-tech industries and market structures produce different probabilities for innovation among small and large firms.[5] Innovation among mainframe computer manufacturers operating in oligopolistic market structures with enormous capital investments typically occurs in large firms. In the far more competitive semiconductor industry, innovations are the products of small and large operations. In fact, small high-tech firms are often able to identify markets or segments ignored by their larger competitors and access these markets quite successfully. Thus, the innovative nature of high-tech industries permits establishments of various sizes to compete in certain product markets. Moreover, traditional dominant firms may be challenged by upstarts and experience at least short-term losses of market shares.

Unique Product Cycles

Unlike most other industries, high-tech industries often exhibit an accelerated product cycle driven by rapid innovation.[6] The time span from initial prototype development to standardized manufacture of a mature product is very limited. In other industries, it is typically the case that a spatial dispersion of production is apparent as a product moves through successive stages of the product cycle. Spatial dispersion may not be as likely for certain high-tech industries that begin new product cycles as quickly as older ones reach maturity. Firms that make rapid adjustments in products and production processes and firms that can generate new products will have the greatest probabilities for success in the high-tech marketplace.

These distinctive characteristics of high-tech industries mean that market composition changes very rapidly as new companies replace others. Many of the new firms are spinoffs of established firms where engineers have identified new products or techniques that compete with or complement those of the parenting company. As new markets open, new and old firms rush in, creating fluctuations in demand, increases in employment, and needs for additional production facilities. As with any competitive industry, this intense competition takes its toll in production suspensions, closed facilities, laid-off employees, and business failures. Surviving firms must also be wary of takeover attempts by larger establishments that have competing product lines or those that are seeking to diversify.[7]

The uncertainty of the environment of high-tech industries, then, can be traced to rapid developments in new technologies and unstable, fragmented market structures. These factors combine to require greater flexibility among high-tech industries than in other industrial sectors. The ways in which high-tech firms have adapted to this uncertain environment and the strategies employed to increase flexibility are not unlike those of other firms in other industries. It is a greater *need* for flexibility that distinguishes high-tech industries.

FLEXIBILITY IN HIGH-TECH ORGANIZATIONS

Tradition, politics, and ideologies play important roles in the decisions about organizational strategies. Research suggests that many U.S. high-tech firms have emulated other domestic industries that have been forced to adapt to newly competitive environments. The typical U.S. response has tended to reflect a short-run, profit-maximizing orientation. Other companies, particularly foreign competitors, have taken more innovative approaches and experimented with alternative organizational structures and novel applications of technology.

Cohen and Zysman in their book, *Manufacturing Matters*, identify these two ideal types of flexibility that shape firms' survival strategies.[8] Dominating the approaches of many U.S. firms is *static flexibility* in which firms react and adjust to market changes in product mix and demand.

> Flexibility has come to mean a whole variety of ways of adjusting company operations to the shifting conditions of the market. The term is used to refer to the ability of a firm to vary efficiently its strategic direction, level of production, composition of goods, length of the work day or week, level of wages, organization of work, or any of a variety of other elements of operations.
>
> The techniques to achieve static flexibility can thus be technological, political, or organizational.[9]

The result of this short-run orientation is that static flexibility tends to produce change in leaps and bounds.

A second type of flexibility is *dynamic flexibility* in which production processes themselves are constantly being redesigned and reorganized and in which products are steadily improved. While a static approach would periodically replace or repair a production system, dynamic flexibility is characterized by proactive improvements and constant adaptations. It involves an investment in research and development as well as a commitment to use and disseminate research and development findings. When production processes are considered in constant evolution, new and innovative ideas can be implemented quickly. As Fred Block says, "At the core of dynamic flexibility is the ability to make rapid use of new technologies."[10] The dynamic approach to flexibility means that productive change is institutionalized. It is a "corporate capacity to develop and introduce these technological advances."[11] Dynamic flexibility is a forward-looking, future-oriented response to the problem of high market uncertainty. Indeed, much of the success of Japanese high-tech firms can be attributed to dynamically flexible production. Static and dynamic approaches to flexibility produce very different managerial responses and productive outcomes. These differences are detailed in the following sections.

STRATEGIES FOR STATIC FLEXIBILITY

Our contention is that static flexibility is reflected in the managerial decisions about organizational structure and production processes of many U.S. high-tech industries, particularly those employing the greatest numbers of workers. Signs of static flexibility can be seen in capital mobility, use of women and minority workers, suppression or avoidance of unions, use of ancillary workers, use of internal and external labor markets, design of the labor process, and limited worker participation in the decision-making processes.

Capital Mobility

One important source of flexibility utilized by high-tech industries and many other industries is geographic movement or capital mobility. By subdividing the production process into standardized components that require limited worker skill to complete, firms can relocate later stages of production to areas where labor costs are lower and/or new markets are emerging. In many cases, the new source of labor may be offshore. While flexibility is gained as a result of deskilling labor and relocating production sites, the results are quite static and fairly permanent. Companies continue to rely on specific machinery and a fairly rigid division of labor that is not easily changed. The emphasis here is on alternative labor sources rather than changes in labor processes.

Capital mobility in high-tech industries became common in the 1960s as foreign competition challenged the U.S. electronics market. Alic and Harris report that while productivity grew in consumer electronics, domestic production employment rapidly declined from 74 percent of all employees to 66 percent.[12] Overall employment in these industries declined from 113,600 in 1974 to 68,400 in 1985. These employment figures are corroborated and extended in our own analysis in the next chapter. Alic and Harris attribute employment declines to the automation of production, better product designs, and the transfer of labor-intensive operations overseas. They argue that driven by increased competition, many consumer electronics companies relocated the production of parts and subassembly operations (an estimated 30,000 jobs or more) overseas to developing countries with low wages.

The labor forces of the microelectronic and computer manufacturing industries were much larger by 1985 than they were in 1974. Yet, according to Alic and Harris, significant reductions in domestic production workers took place over the period. This reduction of production workers can be attributed in part to overseas assembly. Alic and Harris write:

> American semiconductor firms transferred labour-intensive 'back-end' operations overseas—primarily assembly steps such as wire bonding and encapsulation—at a rapid pace beginning in the 1960s. During that decade alone, U.S. companies established more than 50 foreign manufacturing plants. Wafers, fabricated domestically, were shipped to low-wage sites, mostly in Asia, for the final stages in processing, then returned to the United States or sent on to other markets. In recent years, U.S. merchant manufacturers have carried out perhaps 90 percent of all assembly work overseas.[13]

According to Alic and Harris, microelectronic companies halved production costs through outsourcing, resulting in offshore plants with 80 percent of their workers in production jobs while domestic facilities have only 40 percent of their workers in production jobs.

While U.S. employment in computer manufacturing has increased substantially, the proportion of domestic production workers has remained very low (less than 40 percent). The larger numbers of offshore workers are involved primarily in production of peripheral equipment and components (disc drives, keyboards, monitors, and the like). Alic and Harris conclude that corporate rationales for offshore production appear to be locating closer to foreign markets and reducing labor costs to increase profits. Thus, spatial mobility of production has been a major tool for maintaining flexibility among high-tech firms in the semiconductor and computer manufacturing industries. The consequence of this process has been a spatial division of labor that reaches beyond U.S. borders. And, the large proportion of high-skill, technical, and professional jobs in U.S. high-tech industries is in part a consequence of the export of low-skill high-tech production jobs.

Offshore sourcing is not restricted to high-tech manufacturing industries. Service industries involved in high-tech information processing frequently use workers in low-wage domestic and foreign locales for data entry. Occasionally, high-skill jobs are exported to areas where new markets are emerging, but where labor costs remain low. In an interview with one executive vice president of a Fortune 500 software design firm, we were told that there are pockets of highly skilled, often U.S.-trained technical personnel all over the world that are available and eager to work for this company.[14] Indeed, this company has offshore sites in over fifty countries, including Western Europe, the Middle East, Africa, Australia, India, and China. Complex and innovative work in software development can take place almost anywhere. Yet, with a few notable exceptions, most sophisticated, technical innovation continues to be carried out in a handful of research and development enclaves.

We should be quick to note that there is considerable variation within the high-tech sector in capabilities of capital mobility. Only those manufacturing industries in which standardized, mass production is feasible—especially electronics and microelectronics— are likely to relocate production facilities. Likewise, a limited set of service-sector activities are reasonably exportable or otherwise movable. Industries such as medical instruments, communication equipment, and custom electronic equipment do not typically relocate production activities. This is because production is not likely to be standardized or subdivided, markets are for small volumes, and/or constant innovation reduces product cycles and alters production processes.[15] Capital mobility is important as an indicator of static flexibility because the high-tech industries most likely to exhibit geographic dispersion are the largest employers in this advanced sector. In the following section, we turn to another indicator of static flexibility—the use of women and minority workers.

Use of Women and Minority Workers

A two-tiered occupational structure in high-tech industries exhibits an interesting mix of labor market characteristics.[16] The rapidly expanding top tier of management, technical, engineering, and research and development personnel in the United States is congruent with Doeringer and Piore's description of primary labor market jobs—good jobs, high pay, extensive benefits, and avenues for mobility.[17] The labor-intensive production tier of many high-tech firms exhibits classic characteristics of secondary labor market jobs—low-skill, low wages, few benefits, little job security, and limited opportunities for mobility. It is these secondary labor market jobs in which women and, increasingly, racial and ethnic minorities are employed.

As U.S. electronics production jobs have moved offshore, the proportion of women and minorities in domestic high-tech production work has increased.[18] In the United States in 1978, 76 percent of electronics operatives were women, a figure exceeded as the industry increasingly located production offshore.[19] Katz and Kemnitzer report that in Silicon Valley, 45 to 50 percent of the women operatives are third-world immigrants, particularly Asians.[20] In chapter 3, we provide further evidence of the continuing concentration of minorities in operative and assembly jobs in high-tech firms.

High-tech employers are surprisingly candid when asked why women, in particular, comprise such a large segment of the production work force. The rationale appears to be based on sexual stereotypes that attribute greater patience, eye-hand coordination, and manual dexterity to women.[21] Regarding very tedious assembly and inspection work, one employer stated, "You couldn't get a man to stare into a microscope for eight hours a day and do this. They just wouldn't, but the women do it very well. It's not sexual discrimination but physiological and psychological advantages that women have in this work."[22]

Superficial rationale aside, we propose a sociological explanation for the concentration of women and other labor force minorities in menial high-tech jobs. Gender and family roles have important influences on the ways in which individuals participate in the wage-labor system. The traditional ideology that treats men as breadwinners and women as supplemental earners lowers the social value of women's work. Similar traditions surrounding women's family and domestic responsibilities dictate the extent to which they can and "should" work outside the home and shape the opportunities afforded to them in the labor force. These traditions and ideologies lend themselves well to production situations that are organized to minimize skill requirements and that demand flexibility in a work force. Low-skill production positions abound in high-tech industries. Women and minorities accept these low-wage jobs, can be trained fairly quickly, are replaced if they leave, and are more easily laid off if warranted by a drop in product demand. Put simply, minorities and women constitute a flexible labor force that is most attractive to industries that must be most flexible.

In-depth interviews of female assembly workers in the Silicon Valley by Susan Green reveal that these women frequently believe that their virtues of patience and obedience make them better suited to such work than men.[23] Many of those interviewed reported varied and intermittent work histories, and they viewed their current jobs as desirable, particularly in terms of pay and benefits. According to Green, concerns of female high-tech assembly workers center on health and safety issues. Toxic chemicals and fumes, eyestrain, and limited company training or information about health and safety issues are seen as major problems associated with high-tech work. A conclusion drawn from these interviews, however, is that satisfaction with these jobs is relative to perceived employment alternatives. Many other available jobs are no better than high-tech assembly; some are much worse. Green writes:

> Indeed, these are the only kinds of jobs many women in the area can get, especially when reentering the work force after a number of years in the home. In comparison with many of the alternatives—such as cannery work, domestic service, or fast food employment—electronics work appears quite attractive. The industry offers a measure of financial security in a seemingly clean and pleasant environment, and for many women it provides companionship which they do not find as housewives.[24]

Thus, the movement to rural areas of certain high-tech production in the mature stage of a product cycle can be interpreted as an attempt to exploit an available labor supply of women who need supplemental income as family farms decline. One manager of a branch manufacturing plant located in a rural area not far from a high-tech center told us that the location decision was based on the availability of abundant female labor in that area. In nonmetropolitan areas, employment alternatives are often limited, thereby insuring the labor needs of mobile plants.[25] Moreover, the fact that high-tech firms rarely locate research and development centers in rural areas suggests the industry's labor priorities in these location decisions.[26]

The occupational segregation of men and women in high-tech industries is further exaggerated because of men's traditional over-representation in technical engineering and research fields. Occupations defined by the Bureau of Labor Statistics as high-tech include life and physical scientists, mathematical specialists, engineers, engineering and science technicians, and computer specialists. The last three categories compose the largest occupational groups, employing over 90 percent of the workers in high-tech occupations nationally.[27] Each one of these job classifications has traditionally been dominated by white males. While our data indicate women's shares of these fields continue to increase, their overall numbers relative to men continue to be quite small. Others report similar findings. Only seventeen percent of all engineering students were women in 1984, and this number has fallen to between 15 and 16 percent in subsequent years of this decade.[28] Within the electronic components and equipment industry in Santa Clara County, John Keller reports that from 1950 to 1970, women professional and technical workers increased their percentage of the total work force from only 0.9 to 4.0 percent, while men in these occupations increased their share from 18.5 to 30.7 percent.[29]

The segregation of men and women within high-tech occupational groups has also been documented. In a study of computer-related occupations by Glenn and Tolbert, a distinct segregation of occupations by sex was found with men overwhelmingly occupying the higher-skilled computer scientist, programmer, and repair positions and women confined largely to computer operator and data entry positions.[30]

Thus, the particular types of skills and tasks required in the two-tier occupational structure of high-tech industries correspond well to conventional gender stereotypes. Men are found in technical fields and women in detailed, tedious manual work. It is hardly surprising that the division of labor in high-tech industries is often segregated by sex. What may not be anticipated is that the gender segmentation may exceed that in other manufacturing industries. When comparing occupational sex segregation in high-tech and low-tech manufacturing industries, Stearns and Coleman report that segregation is greater in high-tech industries, though declines in segregation from 1973 to 1982 are also greater in these industries.[31] In addition, the study shows that minority women have not enjoyed the same advancements as white women have into prestigious white-collar jobs in high-tech industries.

Other racial and ethnic minorities are increasingly employed in high-tech production in certain labor markets around the country. In a study of the electronics work force at Fairchild Semiconductor Corporation in Santa Clara County from 1961 to 1972, John Keller finds that since 1965 Filipinos, Koreans, Chinese, Indians, and Portuguese have significantly increased their numbers mostly in operative positions. Mexican-Americans and African-Americans are also increasing their shares of the electronics workforce, again in relatively low-skill positions.[32] Keller also cites a study in which is reported: "as many as 83 percent of all professionals and technicians employed in Santa Clara County semiconductor firms are Anglo-American males, whereas half of all unskilled workers in the same firms are minority women."[33] The only racial and/or ethnic minority that appears to have access to more advantaged, technical, and nonproductive positions in high-tech industries is Asian males. Other minorities are largely confined to low-skill jobs in the industry. Keller attributes the influx of women and minority workers into operative positions as a result of a labor shortage in Santa Clara County.

The use of women and racial and ethnic minorities in the production work force of high-tech industries varies by region and labor market area. While Santa Clara County may be an extreme case, our analysis for the years 1970 to 1987 in later chapters indicates that the use of women and minorities in production jobs is fairly universal in U.S. production facilities.

Union Avoidance

Closely allied to the static flexibility strategies of capital mobility and use of women and minority workers is the avoidance of labor unions. High-tech industries are likely to exhibit a flexible labor force that is not encumbered by high union wages, rigid job classification schemes, or job security assurances. Highly competitive market structures and constant fluctuations in supply and demand in many high-tech industries make the flexible use of workers important to high-tech managers. Unions with bureaucratic rules, contractual stipulations, and threats of work stoppages are perceived as inhibiting this requisite flexibility. Thus, high-tech firms are unlikely to be unionized. In the U.S. electronics industry, for example, only 5 percent of workers are unionized. In contrast, the figure for manufacturing workers in all industries is closer to 35 percent.[34]

The chairman of a Fortune 500 manufacturing firm we interviewed asserted, "Unions and high tech just do not go together." He argued that unions destroy initiative and efficiency. Customers of high-tech firms will not stand for work stoppages. Moreover, just-in-time production does not accommodate disruptions in work flow. His own firm had one union plant but, "It just didn't work out. That plant is now a warehouse."[35] The strategies used by this particular company to avoid unions include threats of capital mobility. Another avoidance maneuver involves decentralizing production by reducing plant size (to less than 1000 workers) and building several redundant production establishments. Smaller facilities are thought to be less vulnerable to union organizing than larger ones. Also, frequent meetings are held by management with labor to discuss the drawbacks and dangers of unions for workers.

In an effort to understand the limited success of unionization efforts in high-tech industries, Robinson and McIlwee studied two high-tech companies in the Sunbelt. One is a large firm where personal computers are assembled, and the other is a small branch plant where microelectronic components are manufactured.[36] They found that production work forces of both plants are dominated by women and Hispanics and that the average hourly pay was just above the minimum wage. These researchers identify several factors that contribute to low probabilities of unionization in such plants.

Over half of the workers interviewed said that they would vote for a union if given the opportunity. Yet, for several reasons, such an option is unlikely. Work climates in these firms are very bureaucratic, rule-oriented, and punishment-centered with dismissal used frequently as a control strategy. Frequent evaluations and close supervision are common in these plants, and levels of insecurity among workers are high. The workers have intermittent work histories that include frequent changes among low-wage jobs and extended periods of unemployment and/or other time out of the labor force. Of great interest to these researchers, however, is the political atmosphere of the city in which these plants are located. Situated in a right-to-work state, the city promoted an antiunion and procompany climate in which city officials facilitated repressive control tactics and the manipulation of employees by managers. Votes against unions can clearly flourish in such situations. Indeed, political infrastructures may be as important as internal organizational structures for inhibiting union growth.

As the competition for high-tech firms grows between regions and communities, the supportive climate for these firms and their union avoidance practices is enhanced. That climate often includes antiunion sentiment on the part of political leaders and policymakers and the sanctioning or ignoring of employers' tactics to keep unions out. Union avoidance is yet another important means of generating flexibility.

Ancillary Workers

The use of ancillary workers has also been noted as a static strategy for maintaining organizational flexibility, particularly in high-tech industries. Subcontracting, temporary workers, and a putting-out system of homework have been associated with a variety of high-tech enterprises. A study by Hodson of twelve U.S. high-tech workplaces in a southwestern city reveals extensive and differentiated use of subcontractors by these firms for cafeteria and security work as well as drafting, publishing, marketing, shipping, designing, component testing, assembly, and other special tasks.[37] In this same study, temporary work typically takes the form of clerical or janitorial services, replacements for absent production workers, extra workers needed for production deadlines, and reserve work forces to replace full-time workers who have been dismissed. Hodson finds that part-time workers are of limited use in these high-tech firms because of the extensive amount of training required to do many of the jobs.

In their study of Silicon Valley, Katz and Kemnitzer describe a putting-out system of homework in which high-tech electronic workers are paid on a piece-rate system.[38] The use of homeworkers maximizes flexibility by facilitating additions and deletions to plant work forces. It also allows employers to reduce costs associated with fringe benefits, sick leave, and adherence to safety regulations in the workplace. In terms of social relations in the workplace, homework isolates workers, reducing their opportunities for collective organization. A flexibility strategy not limited to the United States, homework systems are used extensively in other countries, particularly Italy and Spain.[39]

Yet, many prospective workers find the homework system attractive. Katz and Kemnitzer note that some women prefer homework despite the lack of regulation and security associated with it. The workers can more easily adjust work to family demands and their own lifestyle. Moreover, homework can afford greater independence from supervisors in factory settings. Katz and Kemnitzer conclude, "In Silicon Valley, the accompanying ideology emphasizes the close fit with those strands of American culture that stress individual maximization of options for personal success."[40] Our own informal discussions with workers in various high-tech firms suggest that this culture of individualism is supported, cultivated, and exploited in high-tech firms, fostering intense competition among workers for job advancement.

Internal and External Labor Markets

A concept developed in institutional economics, an internal labor market is a set of job opportunities within a firm that resembles a career ladder.[41] In an internal labor market, workers progress up the rungs of the promotional ladder over time, gaining seniority, job security, increased earnings, and new responsibilities. An external labor market is not confined within a single firm. The external career line may include numerous employers and may not reflect an orderly career progression. Some concern has been expressed about the decline in internal labor markets in recent years, and high-tech industries have been a basis for some alarm.[42] In particular, internal labor markets appear to be incongruous with the need for maximum flexibility.

While evidence on high-tech firms' use of internal and external labor markets is inconsistent at this point, the segmentation of labor markets between different levels or tiers of high-tech work appears strongly supported by most research. Stinchcombe and Heimer provide some interesting insights into the use of internal labor markets in the computer software industry.[43] They argue that technical and economic interdependencies develop between firms producing hardware, system programming, applications programming, and mutual clients. These interdependencies can result in exchanges of human capital between firms because of enhanced information flow about employees' expertise and about the availability of positions in participating firms. The product market in the software industry tends toward the imperfect and is described by Stinchcombe and Heimer as "a network of continually reinforced monopolies."[44] Yet, the labor markets associated with technical workers are quite competitive, approaching a more perfect market situation. Thus, a thriving external labor market exists for professional and technical employees. Firms counter with attempts to establish internal labor markets by providing incentives for their most technically talented workers by placing them in important positions on projects and by promoting them to managerial positions. Some firms attempt to retain their very best professionals by including stock options in employee benefit packages. Thus, the development of internal labor markets occurs simultaneously with the development of external markets among software firms.

This analysis of the computer software industry has implications for other high-tech industries. For example, the joint contracting of projects in the space and defense industries involves extensive interorganizational dependencies and interactions that facilitate the transfer of human capital between firms. Employers constantly risk the loss of expertise and technical company secrets. This motivates many firms to provide very attractive economic and promotional opportunity structures as retention devices. The competition for talent and skill is reflected in head-hunting fees, which are rewards for current employees who find bright, new people for a firm to hire. The high-tech research park idea, as an incubator of a localized external labor market, is attractive not only for its clustering of firms for product market advantage, but also for the mobility of technical workers between as well as within firms.

The upper tier of the high-tech occupational structure seems to enjoy the best features of internal and external labor markets. This is not necessarily the case, however, for production workers or clerical staff. Stinchcombe and Heimer point out:

> Neither employers nor employees have much control over the development of human capital among clerical workers such as secretaries and file clerks, because experience is not carefully planned to increase competence, because information about performance is not disseminated, and because career incentives are not systematically offered for the development of such competence. Because engineering companies cannot get competitive advantages through control of excellent clerical workers, they are not very interested in trying to develop or control the human capital of clerical workers; this in turn means that clerical workers themselves do not expect much career advancement from becoming excellent clerical workers.[45]

Production workers in many high-tech firms are also limited in their advancement opportunities. Both Hodson and Green note the limited job mobility of production workers in their case studies of several high-tech industries.[46] Green reports that for the women assemblers she interviewed in the electronics industry, the notion of advancement was more a myth than a reality. College credentials appeared to be a screening device for "technical" work—the next step up from assembly jobs. The technical positions are held less often by women and are rarely occupied by former assemblers. Green states that, although educational opportunities are offered to many assembly workers, job and familial responsibilities frequently prevent them from taking advantage of these benefits. The chairman of a manufacturing firm we interviewed stated that his was the only company of which he knew that offered to pay tuition for any of its employees' courses from "basket weaving to sociology" in order to improve themselves—"as long as they get their work done."[47] It appears that time may be more of a problem than money or other resources for many production workers.

In sum, it seems that production workers and low-level white-collar workers have very limited access to internal labor markets in high-tech firms. Engineers, higher-skilled technical workers, and professionals access internal and external labor markets, maximizing their compensation packages. It is clear that movement between firms by this upper tier of high-tech employees is quite common. The important point is that advancement opportunities for the upper tier are much more available than they are for production or clerical workers. Especially in low-wage locales where production workers are in abundant supply, production jobs in high-tech industries appear to be fairly dead-end. These differences in mobility opportunities suggest important differences in the labor process in high-tech industries.

Design of the Labor Process

While the strategies of capital mobility, avoidance of unions, and use of ancillary workers affect *where* high-tech work will be done, another important issue related to maintaining flexibility is *how* the work will be done. The high-tech workplace often involves very complex production procedures and technologies that change fairly frequently with product shifts or new production techniques. There are several approaches to organizing the production process under these conditions. One strategy, which has been the mainstay of manufacturing in the United States since Henry Ford's first assembly line, is to fragment and routinize the production process, separating planning from execution—a procedure known as scientific management, or Taylorism. The consequences of this approach are a very complex division of labor and a deskilled work force that can be paid low wages and is easily replaceable.

Taylorism limits workers' adaptability to changing products and procedures. In view of the rigidity and complexities of production, it would seem that scientific management would be a less effective approach for organizing work in high-tech industries. Yet, high-tech firms that have been studied in the United States still adhere to most of the tenets of scientific management developed for mass production and mass marketing.

Several studies suggest that high-tech industries employ larger proportions of operatives and low-skill production workers than other manufacturing industries and that high-skill production workers are increasingly likely to be replaced by automation.[48] Research on the Silicon Valley electronics industry reveals assembly work there that is quite labor-intensive and low-skill, involving eye-hand coordination that is difficult to reproduce in automated machinery.[49] Clearly, not all high-tech industry employment involves high-tech occupations. Furthermore, the skill levels of manual occupations in these industries may be quite low. In the short run, low-skill, low-wage, and dispensable workers (often minorities) are useful to firms struggling to keep costs down and profits high. In the long run, however, this strategy locks firms into static flexibility where product innovations occurring in leaps and bounds will likely take precedence over a steadily changing, evolving production process. Within the constraints of a Fordist approach to work organization, adaptations to changing product lines are more likely to include movement and the buying and selling of capital equipment and facilities than alterations of existing plants and production.

In contrast, high-tech industries such as plastics and chemicals employ production strategies that involve more sophisticated, continuous process technologies. A growing body of research suggests that, rather than lowering the skills of workers, continuous process production regimes raise skill levels. In assessing the impact of flexible automation on craft workers and operatives, Fred Block concludes that such technologies tend to increase skill breadth while decreasing skill depth. Furthermore, process technologies ultimately diminish the number of operatives but expand the ranks of the higher-skilled, technical workers.[50] Studies in which workers have been asked to evaluate the effects of high technology on their own skills indicate that the majority feel their skills have been improved. In one of these studies, however, managers appeared less sanguine than workers about skill levels or training results.[51]

Thus, research on production processes in high-tech industries has produced contradictory evidence supporting both deskilling and skill upgrading hypotheses. More often than not, close examination of these mixed findings suggests that they are attributable to differences in industries studied, types of technology used, and/or the manner in which similar technologies are used in different organizational settings. Since technology can clearly be developed and manipulated to require higher- or lower-skill levels of workers, technology plays a central role in the skill levels of workers. The highly specialized machinery of mass production requires limited skill and knowledge on the part of workers. Newer, dynamically flexible machinery, such as numerical control machinery, programmable robots, and computers, requires increasingly skilled operators and has the potential for upgrading skill levels of workers. The latter technology is very expensive in the short run. And, as real wages in the United States have deteriorated in the last two decades, companies have few incentives to adopt the more flexible production technologies. Simply put, statically flexible workers are cheaper than dynamically flexible equipment and facilities.

The distinction in the way technology is used for skill upgrading, skill downgrading, and for organizational flexibility is explicated in an essay by Koppel, Appelbaum, and Albin.[52] These authors describe two alternative organizational designs, "algorithmic" and "robust," that utilize the same computer technologies in very different ways. In algorithmic organizations, computer processes are designed to reduce or eliminate the human element in terms of skill, judgment, and decision-making. In robust firms or units, computers are used to store and process increased information about production that can be accessed by a wide range of workers to evaluate, enhance, or correct ongoing production systems. Workers using this technology require a global rather than fragmented conception of the entire production process. They are involved in an ongoing learning process, improving their skills and increasing their discretion on the job. While algorithmic computer technologies obviously fit neatly among strategies for static flexibility, robust designs open possibilities for dynamic flexibility in the organization of work.

A diversity of production processes from high-tech to low-tech exists within this industrial sector. And, technologies and required skill and knowledge levels vary widely. Political, social, and ideological factors, along with market conditions, organizational traditions, and the nature of the products themselves influence organizational decisions about technology and the organization of work. The preponderance of approaches to flexibility by U.S. high-tech industries can be best characterized as static. The alternative, dynamic flexibility, is the subject of the next section.

STRATEGIES FOR DYNAMIC FLEXIBILITY

The dynamic strategy for organizing work, the opposite of the static approach discussed above, appears less likely to be found among U.S. high-tech industries. Some robust high-tech firms have effectively met the challenges of the uncertain high-tech marketplace by utilizing more flexible, programmable production technology coupled with more broadly trained workers who assume designing as well as functional responsibilities. These firms are more likely to exhibit dynamic flexibility in that workers are constantly involved in the improvement of production processes. New tools can be constantly developed to improve the production process, technologies can be altered to perform different functions as demand dictates, products can be customized to meet specific customer requirements, and new markets can be more easily recognized and developed. Because the machinery used in dynamic approaches is more likely to be alterable to perform different functions, its operators may be trained to acquire the knowledge and skill necessary to reprogram and redesign production equipment. Operators' hands-on knowledge of production becomes extremely important in assessing the viability of new techniques and evaluating old ones. In this context, workers sharpen intellectual skills and broaden the range of applications for their skills.

But dynamic flexibility is not just computerized flexible technology—it is more than that. It is a perspective that mobilizes resources, be they human or machine, in the constant search for new and presumably better ways of doing things. It is inherently a practice of risk-taking since some new ideas may work well while others fail. It is an approach that is as applicable for small start-up firms as it is for large, established companies. However, size and capital may make it more likely to be found in larger firms, more able to survive the failures and false starts inherent in taking such risks. The paradox is that risk-taking varies by industry.[53] It is associated with industry-wide norms, the intensity of competition within an industry, and available technologies. As a result, many large companies in formerly oligopolistic industries, such as automobiles and steel, have been traditionally very conservative players. When confronted with new, foreign competitors who are more willing to regularly develop and implement new ideas, these cautious U.S. firms have suffered the consequences.

In *Work and Politics*, Charles Sabel argues that what we refer to as dynamic work organization is not only more beneficial for workers and employers but inevitable.[54] His argument is based on the erosion of mass markets and increasing production by less-developed countries (LDCs). He reasons that LDCs adopting Fordist production techniques will ultimately be more effective competitors with their U.S. parent firms because wages in these countries can remain much lower than U.S. workers would tolerate. Moreover, as LDCs industrialize, the lag time between innovation and maturity in the product cycle is reduced, allowing less time for innovators to recoup investments before products become obsolete. Finally, as LDCs develop they imitate less and innovate more. While this transformation of LDC production is taking place, wages and standards of living rise in core nations, consumer demand for mass products declines, and demand for custom-made specialty items increases. Thus, LDC manufacturing capacity and changing consumer demand undermine mass markets and production processes of developed nations in the industrial core. Sabel's solution to this dilemma is for core nations to become dynamic, i.e., to innovate and cultivate specialized markets with new products and production technology. On U.S. firms, he argues:

> The strategy of bold innovations raises the chances of their long-term survival on the condition that they radically modify, if not completely abandon, the Fordist principles on which they were built. The manufacture of specialized innovative products requires at least a reinterpretation of Fordist ideas about the nature of markets and the organization of production...[and] the creation of what Fox calls high-trust organizations, organizations in which conception and execution are combined. These are systems in which those who do the work have also determined what work is to be done and how. Such organizations adapt quickly to shifting goals because each worker is able to elaborate incomplete rules and is willing to do so. Able because he understands their connection to the organizations' overarching purposes and to other related routines and willing because, having helped establish the goals, he has a stake in their realization.... The innovative capacity of this firm depends on its flexible use of technology; its close relations with other similarly innovative firms in the same and adjacent sectors; and above all on the close collaboration of workers with different kinds of expertise.[55]

One current example of a dynamic strategy for increased flexibility is rapid applications development (RAD). Large U.S. firms find it increasingly difficult to respond quickly to market changes and moves by competitors. Inflexibility is evident throughout large corporations, including information systems divisions which typically take many months or years to develop applications software for production of new products or modifications of existing lines. RAD is a strategy for streamlining and expediting transformations of corporate management information systems to permit high-speed product development. Proponents of RAD claim that small work teams of developers can yield tenfold increases in productivity compared with traditional corporate applications development departments.[56]

A more well-known application of dynamic flexibility is evidenced by certain Japanese companies that follow the management orientation of Total Quality Control. This means that better quality, as defined by customer satisfaction, is an integral part of work at all levels and in all divisions of the corporation. Through the use of systematic evaluation, scientific methods, and the creation of a work culture with the idea of quality as its core, the continuous improvement of products and production are obtained. This approach exemplifies dynamic flexibility in that change becomes a fundamental feature of the firm.[57]

A dynamic approach seems very congruous with the fast-paced, innovative world of high-tech industries. Yet, in most instances, U.S. high-tech industries do not exhibit much in the way of dynamic work organization. Perhaps the most inflexible characteristics of these firms are implicit fundamental assumptions about capitalist enterprise and labor-management relations. These assumptions are reflected in management's distrust of workers and attempts to deskill, replace, and control them. The tenets are also evident in styles of decision-making that reflect a strong managerial prerogative and a top-down hierarchy of authority. Put simply, management makes policies and workers are obliged to follow them. Yet another fundamental assumption is that the demand for goods is a mass demand and that one line of products will satisfy all consumers. Finally, there is a preoccupation with current problems that result in short-run assessments, short-run solutions, and short-sighted goals. These fundamental assumptions are all contrary to dynamic production, and the contradictions with Sabel's dynamic model are so obvious, that it should come as no surprise that U.S. high-tech industries prefer static strategies of flexible organizations. These styles of management and control in high-tech industries are the subject of the next section.

MANAGERIAL DECISION-MAKING AND CONTROL IN HIGH-TECH ORGANIZATIONS

Static and dynamic flexibility in high-tech firms have important implications for managerial decision-making and control. Static flexibility implies a top-down, Tayloristic management process in which those at the top make policy and those at the bottom execute it. The two-tiered occupational structure, the deskilling of production work, and the spatial separation of different types of workers all facilitate this traditional managerial approach. Dynamic flexibility, on the other hand, implies a more lateral organizational structure. It is assumed that production workers have higher skill and knowledge levels, and that their input is required for continuous improvement of production processes. Thus, the authority hierarchy is more likely to be decentralized, and organizational decision-making reflects a participatory process.

The best way to assess actual decision-making and control strategies used by firms is through case studies. Researchers have encountered substantial resistance, however, in attempting research on high-tech firms. In a study of high-tech firms representing electronics, telecommunications, aerospace, and biotechnology industries, Hodson reports difficulties in gaining access to these firms.[58] Firms that did allow entry by Hodson and his colleagues provide excellent examples of the organizational approaches that seem to dominate many U.S. high-tech industries. It is important to note that most of the firms in this study are parts of very large, established, conglomerates or multinational corporations. While such firms may be in the best position to take risks and apply dynamic techniques, traditional (static) approaches to work organization were found in this research.

Hodson interviewed managers, engineers, and workers in great depth and identified several characteristics of high-tech work organization. Like Robinson and McIlwee, Hodson found that managers claim interest in teamwork, worker participation, and motivation through economic incentives and promotion. Yet, the realities of management practices reveal a different picture. Bureaucratic rules and procedures coupled with close supervision of production workers form the basis of managerial control in these firms. Productivity is largely conceived in terms of individual performance, and time and motion studies—a hallmark of Taylorism—are used to measure productivity. Hodson states, "This treatment of productivity suggests that labor was seen as an interchangeable component of production rather than as a uniquely human entity in need of being motivated to do quality work."[59] Workers have no clearly defined, formal procedures for participating in workplace decisions. At best, worker contributions in this regard are informal and typically take the form of suggestions. Mobility opportunities for production workers are very limited and movement tends to be lateral rather than upward. This is particularly true for women in high-tech firms who are quite outspoken on the mobility issue. Mobility among engineers in larger firms typically means changing firms, and Hodson found turnover rates high among all employees with the exception of first-line supervisors. In contrast, he reports considerably lower turnover rates among workers in smaller organizations.

Hodson also found evidence of managerial incompetence. One source of incompetence is that managers are too far removed from production and do not understand the complexities of rapidly changing, high-tech production processes. A second source of incompetence stems from workers' perceptions that managers obtain their positions through favoritism and social networks rather than through knowledge and competence. Both workers and engineers alike expressed concern about managerial incompetence and identified this problem as a major source of work dissatisfaction. A third source of managerial incompetence we have encountered in our research is that technically trained managers may not have any human relations skills. As a result, their styles tend to be less professional and more authoritarian. Hodson concludes from his interviews that there appears to be a crisis of organizational structure and managerial competence among the firms that he studied. He writes:

> The causes of this crisis appear to reside in too-rapid technological change, insufficient genuine participation for workers, and unmediated management power. The consequences of this crisis are a tremendous discrepancy between stated agendas and actual practices in areas ranging from internal labor markets to quality control, to measuring productivity, to participative management. This crisis is all the more significant because it is occurring in core industrial sectors that are highly significant to the overall health of the economy.[60]

This lack of confidence in management has been documented in other case studies of high-tech firms. Kaufman and co-workers found in their case study of an "ultra-high-tech" firm that a major source of job dissatisfaction among a sample of employees at various skill levels related to managerial practices and policies.[61] These issues included management indecision and vacillation, company politics, lack of accountability, communication problems, and other unspecified concerns. These researchers conclude that in high-tech firms organizational structure and change are as important as technology in their impact on workers and work outcomes.

A third case study indicative of managerial problems in high-tech firms is that of Bielby and co-workers who conducted simulations of decision-making processes among managers and professionals in a Silicon Valley high-tech firm.[62] These researchers found that engineers, as a result of technical expertise, have more power in high-tech firms and that their technical values are often at odds with business goals. This results in barriers to communication and cooperation in decision-making between technical and business personnel. We should add, however, that these researchers also found that dominant groups are able at times to subordinate their own goals in favor of organizational objectives.

From these and other case studies of high-tech firms, it appears that management problems may be critical for many high-tech industries. The separation of management from the production process appears to be at the root of many of the problems identified above. It is a common practice among high-tech firms to segregate production workers from highly skilled technicians, engineers, and professionals. The fear seems to be that the freedom and autonomy of engineers and professionals might erode the discipline and efficiency of production workers. With this contingency control strategy, those designing technologies and products become removed from those who carry out the production on a daily basis.

In top-down managerial hierarchies of high-tech firms there are few direct or systematic ways for workers to communicate problems or ideas encountered in production to system designers. High-tech products and production systems are constantly being transformed, and information flow between higher and lower levels is critical. Without adequate communication, the success of a strategy of dynamic flexibility is surely improbable. Thus, despite the obvious need for fluid decision-making structures, it appears that the majority of U.S. high-tech manufacturing industries have adopted a more traditional strategy of top-down authority, autocratic decision-making, and segregation of skill levels with contingency control techniques (autonomy for engineers and strict discipline for production workers). The chairman of a major high-tech manufacturing firm we interviewed proudly and emphatically stated that there are few meetings, no committees, and no decision-making by consensus in his company. One person makes the decision and that person is held responsible for the consequences.[63]

We do not mean to imply that all high-tech firms are rigidly authoritarian in their management styles. Many high-tech firms in the United States have attempted to incorporate more group processes, worker participation, and bottom-up decision-making if for no other reason than to dissuade workers from collective organization. However, many unworkable contradictions have been documented when high-tech firms try to combine democratic organization with traditional hierarchical structures. Experimental projects tend to be abandoned when production crunches arise or when they are so successful that managerial positions are threatened.[64] Citing their firms' insecurity and market fluctuations, managers in high-tech firms often argue that long-term innovative management attempts are not feasible. More often than not, worker participation in many high-tech firms may only be temporary and more symbolic than real.

Without these more consensual, democratic, and/or participatory structures, the likelihood of incorporating dynamic flexibility into high-tech organizations is minimized. In the short-run, many high-tech firms are achieving economic success with a traditional organizational structure, building flexibility through new products, relocating production facilities, avoiding unions, hiring women and minority production workers, segmenting labor markets, and deskilling workers. What may be in a high-tech firm's short-run interest, however, may not be in the long-run interest of a local or national economy. We agree with Cohen and Zysman that dynamic flexibility may be imperative for the United States to restructure the economy successfully and maintain a major position in the international marketplace of the twenty-first century. Yet, the purpose of this book is to recount the current standing of high-tech industry workers in light of the static measures taken by management. In the next section, we consider the implications of high-tech industry employment for the socioeconomic standing of workers.

IMPLICATIONS FOR INEQUALITY

It is our contention that the nature of the high-tech labor process and the way in which it is organized in labor markets and firms have definite implications for economic and social inequality within high-tech industries. Employment trends that accompany the static flexibility approach would suggest that inequality between the top and bottom employees of high-tech industries is great and shows no signs of waning. Economic inequality in high-tech industries derives largely from a two-tiered occupational structure that differentiates professional and technical workers from operative and assembly workers. Offshore sourcing and capital mobility may reduce numbers and proportions of production workers in particular locations, reducing economic inequality levels in those areas. But rather than eradicating disparities, this strategy exports the inequality between the top and bottom occupational levels to other locations. As we shall see in the subsequent analyses, with less permeable opportunity structures, economic inequality in high-tech industries becomes tied to gender, race, and ethnic segmentation more so than in other industries. Similarly, inequality is exacerbated by the increasing use of ancillary production workers in high-tech industries. Many of the economic benefits enjoyed by high-tech workers in traditional factory settings are not shared by their homework or temporary work counterparts. To the extent that labor is deskilled to cut costs and to reduce employers' uncertainties, the gap between the top and bottom tiers of high-tech employees will widen. Moreover, deskilling and certain applications of automation restrict mobility opportunities for the bottom tier of production workers. These manifestations of static flexibility in high-tech firms can only serve to entrench or increase economic inequality within high-tech industries.

Social inequality in high-tech firms is also likely. The organizational strategies described above have implications for inequalities in power, authority, autonomy, job satisfaction, and alienation. Through the separation and segregation of two tiers of high-tech workers by autocratic decision-making and contingency control tactics, the gulf between professional/technical workers and production workers is maintained, if not widened. When mobility opportunities for production workers are limited, these inequalities become entrenched structural features of the high-tech organization of work.

An alternate work organization, dynamic production, should have the opposite implications for both economic and social inequality. Production workers' skills are upgraded, providing more opportunities for them to contribute to design and decision-making and reducing the barriers between high- and low-skill jobs. This, in turn, could reduce possibilities for the kind of segmentation along race, ethnic, or gender lines that has been found in many U.S. high-tech industries. Because production is not as labor-intensive, low-skill or fragmentable, dynamic organization also makes capital mobility a less viable option for increasing profits or cutting costs.

Our depiction of U.S. high-tech industries in this chapter is drawn largely from case studies of electronics firms and high-tech centers such as Silicon Valley. A major problem we must confront in relying on these studies is that they do not represent or exhaust the variety or complexity of high-tech industries, firms, jobs, and labor markets. To be sure, the electronics industry comprises a major share of employment in high-tech industries. In our definitional scheme, however, there are several other manufacturing industries, including computers, chemicals, communications, and plastics. Any of these industries may involve very different work organizations, production processes, technologies, firm characteristics, and management strategies. Moreover, as we shall see in the following chapter, the electronics industry is losing its position as the foremost provider of domestic high-tech jobs. When we include high-tech service industries in our sectoral model, dramatic departures from the conventional electronics scenario are possible.

In the chapters that follow, we will study the extent to which various high-tech industries and various high-tech locales appear to resemble or contradict the image of static flexibility and inequality that we have sketched in this chapter. While the analyses are on an industry level and prevent us from ascertaining firm-specific organizational designs and strategies, this level of analysis allows us to examine variation within the high-tech sector utilizing large, generalizable samples of U.S. workers. In chapter 3, we focus on the development and current status of the U.S. high-tech industrial labor force. We then turn to the implications of a high-tech presence in local economies and labor markets in chapters 4 and 5.

Chapter Three

Employment in High-Tech Industries: Technical and Social Divisions of Labor

In this chapter we trace the development of employment in U.S. high-tech industries since 1970. We focus first on the technical division of labor, i.e., the differential composition of the occupational structures of high-tech industries. We then turn to the social division of labor based on race, gender, and ethnicity. In sketching the emergence of high-tech employment, we find it useful to contrast this relatively new form of work with the traditional manufacturing sector and with the burgeoning service sector. It is also illustrative to examine trends for specific industries and segments within the high-tech sector.

We highlight a number of trends from which we infer evidence of static or dynamically flexible production. For example, we pay close attention to evidence of a shrinking blue-collar component in the U.S. high-tech industrial labor force. We interpret that as an indication of production rearrangements that include capital mobility and automation, reflecting a static approach to flexible production. We also examine high-tech industries' use of minority workers. If vulnerable labor force participants are generally confined to the least desirable jobs in the high-tech sector, we interpret this as a sign of static flexibility as well. We also examine the extent to which a two-tiered occupational structure exists in the high-tech sector as a whole and within specific industries. The occupational tiers are contrasted in terms of minority composition as we examine the intersection of the technical and social divisions of labor. As we shall see, there is considerable evidence that employers struggling to meet the demands of volatile high-tech markets tend to adopt statically flexible production strategies.

The notion of static flexibility embodies important implications for the future organization of work. Paramount among these would

41

be necessary changes in expectations about employment opportunities and security. Employment in a rapidly growing industry, particularly a manufacturing industry, has long been associated with job stability, chances for advancement, and high wages. If signs of static flexibility distinguish high-tech industries that are large employers, much of the optimism about these sunrise industries must be tempered by the reality of work organization within them. As we shall see, there are clear parallels between the developing high-tech industrial sector and its traditional industrial counterparts. New industries do not necessarily depart from old patterns of work organization. In the analysis that follows, we hope to demonstrate ways in which the high-tech sector and other industrial sectors have converged and diverged over the last two decades.

DATA SOURCES

The primary data source for our depiction of the development of the high-tech industry labor force is the monthly Current Population Survey (CPS) conducted by the U.S. Bureau of the Census. From the surveys for the years 1970 through 1987, we have extracted data on 1.6 million labor force participants.[1] This master file is large enough to provide reliable, representative annual estimates of the size of the high-tech industrial sector, including numbers of minority workers. The sample size also allows us to focus on some of the larger industries and segments within the technology sector.

The data do not include information on specific firms or social relations of production in particular workplaces. As we argued in the second chapter, these phenomena are best investigated with a case study approach. The CPS survey is designed to produce national estimates of employment and unemployment, and precise geographic designations cannot be made with these data. When we focus on specific locales in the fourth and fifth chapters, we necessarily turn to other census data designed for geographic detail. Nonetheless, the CPS data provide a very useful basis for outlining the national development of the high-tech industry labor force since 1970.

DEFINITION OF HIGH-TECH INDUSTRIES

In the first chapter, we discussed at length the definition of high-tech industries employed here. It is based on the widely used scheme developed by the Bureau of Labor Statistics (BLS). The BLS definition relies on industry levels of scientific and technical workers and on levels of research and development expenditures. Manufacturing industries include guided missiles, spacecraft, ordnance, communications equipment, office and computing machinery, drugs, chemicals, and the like. To the set of manufacturing industries defined as high-tech by the BLS, we add a handful of service industries suggested by Malecki. These industries are distinct from other service industries in that their occupational structures are dominated by professional and technical workers. It is also the case that product orientations and close linkages to innovative manufacturing clearly resemble high-tech manufacturing industries. Computer software development, for example, is a highly technical service industry that is integrally linked to computer hardware manufacturing. Thus, we include high-tech manufacturing and service industries of this sector.

THE RISE OF EMPLOYMENT IN HIGH-TECH INDUSTRIES

Employment growth in the high-tech industrial sector has been strong since the mid-1970s. The rapid expansion of this sector has been noted by Rumberger and Levin and by Riche, Hecker, and Burgan among others.[2] Those same writers caution quite correctly that the rapid growth of high-tech industry employment is not likely to have a major impact on total U.S. job growth any time soon. We illustrate this important caveat with CPS data on U.S. labor force participants in Figure 3.1.[3] As the graph suggests, the U.S. labor force has expanded by 45 percent since 1970. And in that same time frame, the high-tech industrial sector has increased by about 50 percent. The strong high-tech growth rate notwithstanding, the actual number of such jobs continues to be a small part (about 6 percent) of the national employment picture. Indeed, despite the rapid growth of high-tech industrial employment, the service sector has increased its share of aggregate employment by almost 60 percent.[4] These data cast considerable doubt on the ability of the high-tech sector to absorb workers displaced from other manufacturing industries in which employment grew only 2 percent from 1970 to 1987.

   With these cautions about the numbers of high-tech jobs in mind, we next turn to CPS data on growth among the 16 detailed industries we have classified as high-tech. The data in Table 3.1 indicate numbers of workers in different high-tech industries, while Figure 3.2 illustrates proportional changes from 1970 to 1987.[5] The data

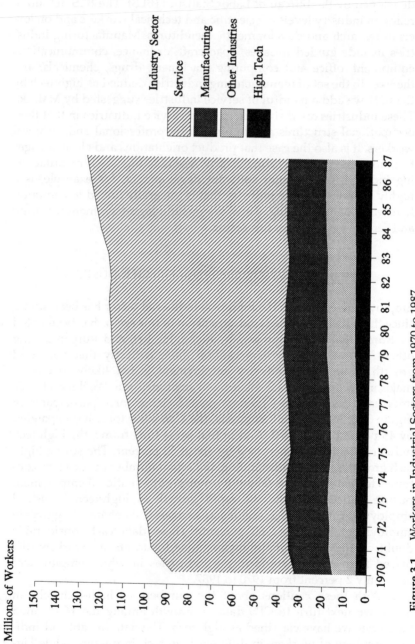

Millions of Workers

Industry Sector

Service

Manufacturing

Other Industries

High Tech

1970 71 72 73 74 75 76 77 78 79 80 81 82 83 84 85 86 87

Figure 3.1 Workers in Industrial Sectors from 1970 to 1987

in the table and the figure indicate little uniformity in the growth patterns among the various industries we classify as high technology. One important source of variability in the annual industry estimates is due to sampling error among smaller industries. We will avoid making generalizations about such volatile data as those associated with an industry like plastics and synthetics. A more important source for the apparent lack of uniformity is the fact that the period from 1970 to 1987 was one of substantial transition within the high-tech sector. Newer industries grew and diversified while mature industries remained constant or declined. At the earliest point in the data series, the electrical machinery, equipment, and supplies industry category accounted for 25 percent of all high-tech sector employment. While that industry continued to be the largest high-tech employer in 1987, its share of the sectoral labor force declined slightly to 21 percent. This decline in high-tech employment share occurred despite a 33 percent increase in the size of the electrical machinery industry.

Other high-tech manufacturing industries exhibit substantial growth. These include guided missiles, space vehicles, ordnance, electronic computing equipment, and scientific instruments. The expansion of the guided missiles, spacecraft, and ordnance industries evident in the data is no doubt a product of the defense buildup of the 1980s. The rise of high-tech services (testing labs, business and management consulting, and computer services and software) is another obvious feature of these data. By 1987, these once inconsequential industries accounted for 20 percent of all high-tech employment. Moreover, U.S. workers in high-tech service industries doubled the number working in computer manufacturing, despite the latter industry's significant growth. This last observation bears repeating: more than twice as many high-tech workers were employed in services as in computer manufacturing.

Perhaps the most noteworthy decline detailed in Table 3.1 is that of the radio, TV, and communications equipment industry. Employment decreased 19 percent across the period, and the radio-TV industry's share of U.S. high-tech employment declined from 13 to 6 percent. By 1987, the aircraft manufacturing industry exhibited 12 percent fewer workers that it did in 1970. These changes in industry-specific labor forces will make an interesting context for an examination of industrial occupation composition in a subsequent section. Surely the notion that the U.S. high-tech sector is a rapidly growing component of the labor force is an oversimplification. Such an observation belies substantial heterogeneity within the sector. Some industries are in an

Table 3.1 High-Tech Industry Employment from 1970 to 1987 (in thousands)

Year	Plastics	Drugs and Medicine	Chemicals	Spacecraft, Missiles	Engines and Turbines	Office Equip.	Computers	Radio, TV, and Communications
1970	141	155	396	250	119	178	184	601
1971	187	178	428	228	102	146	196	601
1972	182	173	485	263	106	154	195	709
1973	209	207	483	247	102	150	225	698
1974	248	197	470	212	94	137	247	632
1975	184	187	517	203	124	166	246	603
1976	211	212	588	187	111	119	287	529
1977	170	209	573	197	111	137	330	594
1978	181	179	621	212	123	147	404	719
1979	196	214	686	231	149	160	446	663
1980	209	234	648	255	139	155	517	721
1981	165	226	559	253	124	164	569	665
1982	158	221	645	326	141	167	618	645
1983	161	183	545	406	112	110	659	596
1984	124	235	603	472	87	111	761	555
1985	109	253	631	525	88	103	737	575
1986	132	274	587	520	96	76	621	665
1987	142	259	598	541	87	104	793	488
% change	0.9	66.5	50.8	116.4	-26.8	-41.9	332.2	-18.7

Table 3.1 (*continued*)   High-Tech Industry Employment from 1970 to 1987 (in thousands)

Year	Electrical Machinery	Aircraft	Scientific Instruments	Optical and Health	Photographic Equipment	R&D Test Labs	Business Consulting	Computer Services
1970	1192	777	125	139	84	131	192	94
1971	1253	613	185	170	124	103	216	99
1972	1248	558	169	190	99	88	229	97
1973	1432	567	208	170	122	109	223	123
1974	1402	529	201	200	124	125	254	123
1975	1384	560	189	202	134	128	261	104
1976	1386	553	160	216	160	144	298	114
1977	1508	570	158	229	156	142	346	127
1978	1603	655	211	274	151	146	332	189
1979	1756	646	173	300	167	189	346	229
1980	1756	644	224	287	162	166	447	243
1981	1725	672	212	254	166	194	478	281
1982	1483	653	264	262	143	247	472	371
1983	1533	608	268	267	106	248	522	453
1984	1628	651	239	309	150	202	431	494
1985	1526	685	253	325	152	215	553	579
1986	1578	751	245	302	113	256	526	700
1987	1586	680	302	275	151	272	615	657
% change	33.1	-12.5	141.3	98.1	79.0	107.5	220.8	601.9

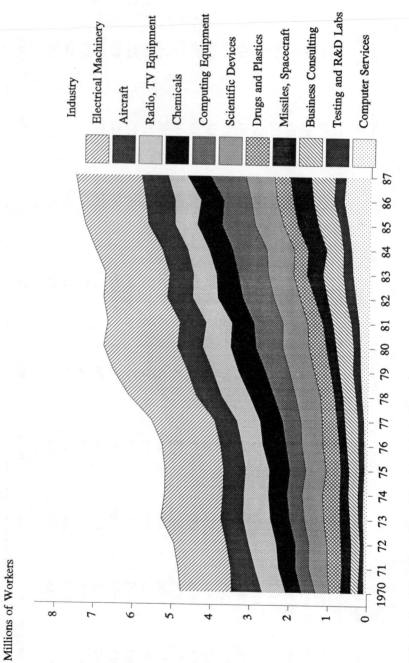

Millions of Workers

Industry

Electrical Machinery
Aircraft
Radio, TV Equipment
Chemicals
Computing Equipment
Scientific Devices
Drugs and Plastics
Missiles, Spacecraft
Business Consulting
Testing and R&D Labs
Computer Services

Figure 3.2 Workers in High-Tech Industries from 1970 to 1987

accelerated domestic employment expansion and others in a long-term employment contraction.

In sum, high-tech industry employment was a prominent feature of national employment during the 1970s and 1980s. It is important, however, not to be overly sanguine about the ability of the high-tech sector to create jobs in numbers that will rival the service sector or other manufacturing industries that may be in decline. It should also be noted that employment expansion among high-tech industries is occurring at varying rates and may lead to an important reconstitution of work opportunities within the sector. Perhaps the most interesting aspect of work organization in high-tech industries is a two-tiered occupational structure. In the following section, we employ CPS data to examine the development and current status of the high-tech occupation structure.

THE CHANGING HIGH-TECH TECHNICAL DIVISION OF LABOR

In this period of growth, the occupational mix of high-tech industries changed in important ways. To illustrate this, we draw on occupational data in the CPS to assess trends among four occupation groups: managerial, administrative, professional, and technical workers; other clerical and sales white-collar workers; precision production workers; and blue-collar workers.[6] Data for each of these occupational categories are displayed in Figure 3.3 where the bars represent occupational distributions of high-tech workers and the lines correspond to workers in all other industries. In the early 1970s, blue-collar workers constituted almost 40 percent of employment in the high-tech sector and just over 40 percent in other industries. The blue-collar occupation group is the largest component of the high-tech occupation structure, and the management, professional, and technical group—fully 10 percent smaller—is a distant second. This pattern has reversed substantially since 1980. By 1987, the percentage of high-tech blue-collar workers was down 15 percent from 1973, and the percent of management, professional, and technical workers was up roughly the same amount. We surmise that this blue-collar employment decline is due principally to increasing offshore production and automation. It should be noted that other industries exhibit a decline in blue-collar workers, but that decrease is not nearly as great as that of high-tech industries. The trends of high-tech and other industries diverge significantly over time.

The proportion of high-tech workers employed in precision production remains relatively constant and slightly higher than the same

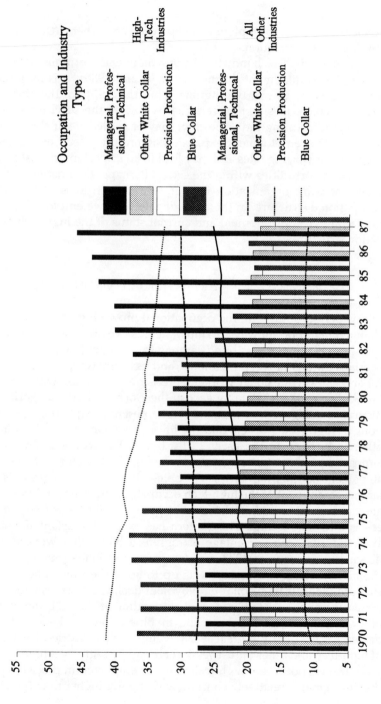

Percent

Figure 3.3   Occupational Composition by Sector from 1970 to 1987

proportion of workers in other industries. While high-tech blue-collar employment declines substantially in Figure 3.3, other white-collar employment decreases only slightly. In 1970, other white-collar clerical and sales high-tech employment was about 7 percent lower than in other industries, but by 1987 the difference approached 12 percent. High-tech industries clearly employ fewer middle-level, white-collar workers.

The most pronounced contrast between high-tech and other industries' occupational distributions is evident among managerial and professional workers. On the average, high-tech industries consistently employ more managers and professionals than other industries throughout the 1970–1987 period. While we might expect technologically intensive industries to employ proportionately more scientists, engineers, and technicians, the gap between the high-tech sector and other industries increases greatly across time. Early in the 1970s, high-tech industries were composed of about 8 percent more managers and professionals than other industries. By 1987, high-tech industries employed 20 percent more managers and professionals than other industries.

Thus, the occupational mix of high-tech industries has come to be very different from those of other industries. The kinds of changes evident here are somewhat consistent with theories of a shrinking middle class that posit a growing loss of secure, well-paying clerical and production jobs.[7] We characterize the high-tech occupation structure as two-tiered. By that we mean that the occupational composition is increasingly top-heavy, creating a sharper contrast among salaried, autonomous management; administrative, professional, and technical workers; and all other high-tech workers. Indeed, the trends in Figure 3.3 suggest that U.S. high-tech employment may eventually become a single tier of highly skilled managers and professionals. In the interim, we demonstrate in subsequent analyses the paradoxical social and economic consequences of working in a declining lower tier of a growing industrial sector.

Table 3.2 affords a more detailed view of the changing technical division of labor in high-tech industries. In the table, data for the same four occupational categories are presented for each industry in 1970 and again in 1987. We identify two major characteristics of these data that are used to classify high-tech industries into homogeneous groupings based on their respective technical divisions of labor: (1) the occupational distribution of blue-collar and white-collar workers, and (2) the change in this distribution from 1970 to 1987. These features are a useful way to group the sixteen high-tech industries into segments that may reflect one facet of static or dynamically flexible production strategies. The resulting four categories or segments of high-tech industries include the primarily white-collar service industries and three groups of manufacturing industries.

In Table 3.2, rapidly expanding service industries have an occupational composition most dominated by white-collar positions. The administrative, management, professional, and technical occupational category for these industries increased by 11 to 18 percent. At the same time, the clerical and sales component (other white-collar) declined by at least 15 percent in two of the service industries. The elimination of clerical workers evident in the service high-tech industries is most likely a function of the increased use of computers and expert systems. The occupational composition of service high-tech industries is so distinctive in its white-collar configuration that we treat the services as a discrete segment of the high-tech sector and conduct separate analysis of them in most cases below.

Among high-tech manufacturing industries, drugs, guided missiles and spacecraft, and computing equipment exhibited large proportional increases in white-collar workers. The upper tiers of these fast-growing industries exhibit percentage increases ranging from 13 to 26 percent. By 1987, white-collar workers dominated the domestic occupational structures of these industries. The same industries show double-digit percentage reductions in other blue-collar jobs. While similar to high-tech service industries in exhibiting large percentage increases in upper-tier jobs, drugs, guided missiles and spacecraft, and computing equipment differ from the services with distinct proportional declines in domestic blue-collar jobs. When we find it useful to group high-tech industries into segments below, we refer to these industries as white-collar manufacturing industries.

The data in Table 3.2 also indicate that several high-tech industries maintained sizeable blue-collar labor forces but reduced proportions of less-skilled labor from 1970 to 1987. Plastics, industrial chemicals, office machines, radio and TV equipment, electrical machinery, aircraft, optical and health instruments, and photographic equipment generally show relatively smaller increases in upper-tier components and virtually the same proportion of blue-collar workers. It is important to note, however, that the precision production component of the lower tier of these industries tended to increase while other blue-collar employment declined. This is strongly suggestive of static flexibility strategies such as outsourcing of assembly and similar operative jobs. Had other blue-collar jobs increased in these industries at rates comparable to other types of employment, these industries would

Table 3.2   Occupational Composition of High-Tech Industries in 1970 and 1987 (in thousands)

Industry	Administration, Management, Professional, and Technical				Other White-Collar				Precision Production				Other Blue-Collar			
	1970		1987		1970		1987		1970		1987		1970		1987	
	N	%	N	%	N	%	N	%	N	%	N	%	N	%	N	%
Plastics and synthetics	30	21	41	29	15	10	25	17	25	18	16	12	71	50	60	42
Drugs and medicines	43	28	118	46	53	34	67	26	13	8	33	13	47	30	40	16
Industrial chemicals	94	24	220	37	84	21	115	19	46	12	107	18	172	43	155	26
Guided missiles, spacecraft	61	25	275	51	39	16	95	18	55	22	80	15	91	37	91	17
Engines & turbines	22	19	30	35	21	17	5	6	32	27	10	12	44	37	42	48
Office equipment	46	26	40	39	58	33	28	27	22	12	20	20	52	29	15	14
Computers	81	44	454	57	24	13	136	17	24	13	64	8	55	30	139	18
Radio, TV, communications equipment	158	26	235	48	110	18	80	16	88	15	101	21	246	41	72	15
Electrical machinery	199	17	494	31	216	18	239	15	139	12	447	28	638	54	406	26
Aircraft	243	31	242	36	136	17	91	13	198	25	178	26	200	26	168	25
Scientific instruments	40	32	118	39	33	26	50	17	20	16	40	13	32	26	94	31
Optical and health instruments	32	23	84	31	21	15	49	18	21	15	42	15	65	47	100	36
Photographic equipment	31	37	59	39	21	25	26	18	12	14	31	21	21	25	34	23
Testing, R&D labs	74	56	187	69	43	33	47	17	7	5	16	6	7	6	22	8
Business consulting	115	60	440	72	69	36	163	27	0	0	1	0	8	4	10	2
Computer services	46	49	440	67	42	45	172	26	3	3	37	6	3	3	7	1

employ many more blue-collar workers in 1987 than they did in 1970. Still, in contrast to the services and white-collar manufacturing industries, the blue-collar component of these high-tech industries continues to approach one-half of all employment. Thus, we refer to this group of industries as the mixed manufacturing segment. As the data in the table suggest, this segment is the largest of all, employing roughly one-half of all high-tech workers.

Like the mixed manufacturing group, the remaining two industries in Table 3.2—engines and turbines and scientific instruments—maintain very high percentages of blue-collar workers (over 40 percent). Unlike all other high-tech industries, however, these two industries registered large *increases* in low-skill other blue-collar employment from 1970 to 1987. Taking precision production employment into account as well, we note that engines and turbines and scientific instruments are the only industries to have larger lower tiers in 1987 than in 1970. These data are quite suggestive of deskilling—the simplification and routinization of work. We contend that deskilling is another characteristic feature of static flexibility. Though the engines and turbines and scientific instruments industries comprise a very small category, we believe the trends of development differ enough to warrant separate treatment at several points in our analysis. We refer to them as the blue-collar manufacturing segment of the high-tech sector.

The trends in Table 3.2 are summarized in Figure 3.4 for the four high-tech industry segments we have identified here. The growth of the service and white-collar manufacturing industry segments from 1970 to 1987 is clearly apparent. A most striking feature of that growth is that much of the expansion took place in upper-tier employment. For the mixed manufacturing segment, the figure demonstrates the consistency of the lower tier of production workers as well as the compositional change within it. While precision production jobs increased by 1987, other blue-collar jobs declined. The figure also documents the small but proportionately large growth in other less-skilled blue-collar employment for the blue-collar manufacturing segment.

To summarize, the technical division of high-tech industry labor generally features what we label a "two-tier structure." That is, one large, growing component of administrative, professional, and technical workers and a modest, typically declining component of blue-collar workers. When we examine segments within high-tech industries, however, we find several patterns of occupational composition and change. These differences within the sector suggest that, while static forms of flexibility are the norm, there are some industries where

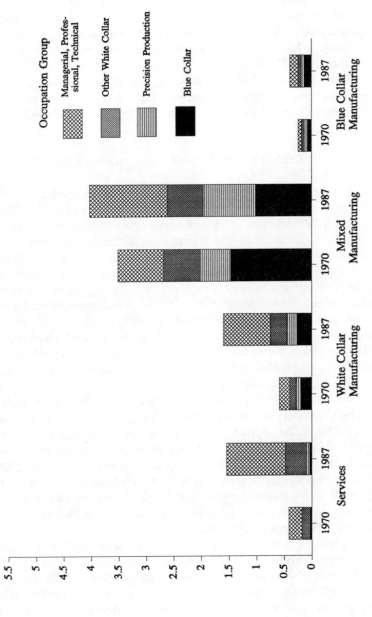

Figure 3.4   Occupational Distributions by Industry in 1970 and 1987

dynamic approaches may succeed. Among high-tech industries, the services and white-collar manufacturing groups exhibit the most occupational upgrading across time and may be in the best position to employ dynamic strategies. The blue-collar manufacturing group with its increase in low-skill employment may be most prone to static flexibility measures. Those measures may lead to a loss of blue-collar jobs not unlike that exhibited by mixed high-tech manufacturing industries. With this depiction of the technical division of labor in mind, we next consider social divisions based on race, gender, and ethnicity.

THE SOCIAL DIVISION OF HIGH-TECH LABOR

A two-tier technical division of labor in high-tech industries is often justified in terms of the advanced skill requirements of production in that sector. Much of the work demands highly trained engineers, scientists, and technicians. And if access to the high-tech occupational structure is not governed by basic social divisions such as race, gender, and ethnicity, the two-tier technical division of labor could simply be viewed as a necessary technical artifact of production in that sector. Indeed, the transformation of the high-tech occupational distribution could be a welcome upgrading of job opportunities for all categories of workers. Driven by market pressures and shortages of skilled technical labor, the high-tech sector could be one of the few industrial groups that cannot afford to discriminate on the basis of race, gender, and/or ethnicity.

Such an upgrading would reflect a dynamic flexibility strategy in which workers are redeployed in increasingly technical assignments. This redistribution could include retraining and reskilling of an industrial labor force composed of large numbers of women, blacks, and other minority labor force participants. Yet, we find little evidence of dynamism among U.S. high-tech industries. Instead, the high-tech sector exhibits signs of static flexibility such as labor outsourcing, offshore production, union avoidance, and exploitation of minority labor force participants.

A key requirement of a static flexibility approach is the reliance on a flexible production labor force that can be shaped to meet the demands of just-in-time production. Competitiveness in the static perspective means reduction of production costs, most notably labor. One way to minimize costs is to employ vulnerable workers who labor for low wages and who have few other comparable employment opportunities. The control of labor costs then becomes a process of regulating the employment of vulnerable workers. In the United States, few social attributes increase workers' vulnerability more than gender, race, and ethnicity. In the analysis that follows, we examine minority labor force participation in high-tech industries.

We use the term "minority" in the conventional sociological sense. That is, we use the concept to refer to groups that possess relatively less autonomy, power, and control than other groups. These less powerful groups may or may not exist in numerical minority in relation to other, more powerful groups. In the context of high-tech industries, we operationalize minority labor force participants as women, blacks, and Hispanics. The Census data we use identify a racial category called "other" that primarily includes persons of Asian descent. Our preliminary analysis and the research of others suggest that men in the other category are employed in high-tech industries in ways very similar to white males. Thus, our approach treats white and other males as nonminority labor force participants. White females, women of color, and men of color except those coded as other are classified as minorities.

The percentages of minority labor force participants in high-tech and all other industries are presented in Figure 3.5 for the years 1970 to 1987. The trends indicate that there are proportionately fewer minorities employed in high-tech industries throughout the period. In 1970, minority labor force participants constituted 37 percent of high-tech industry workers. A small increase is evident such that by 1987 just over 40 percent of high-tech workers were minorities. Other industries employed substantially more minority workers. Indeed, white and other males became a numerical minority in the balance of the labor force during the period under scrutiny. Some convergence of high-tech and other industry patterns is evident until 1980 at which point the trends appear to diverge. While high-tech industries exhibit some increase in minority labor force participants, the sector clearly differs from the pattern of other industries. We might add that this divergence may well be attributed to the dramatic increase in white-collar professionals indicated above. This is an occupational group composed largely of white males and relatively few minority workers. We will develop this point further in the next section.

Details on social division of high-tech industry labor are given in Figure 3.6. The data indicate that, while the sector as a whole expanded, minority labor force participants were incorporated into high-tech industries at a faster rate than white males. Though they outnumbered all other gender, racial, and ethnic groups throughout the period, white males exhibited the least percentage change from

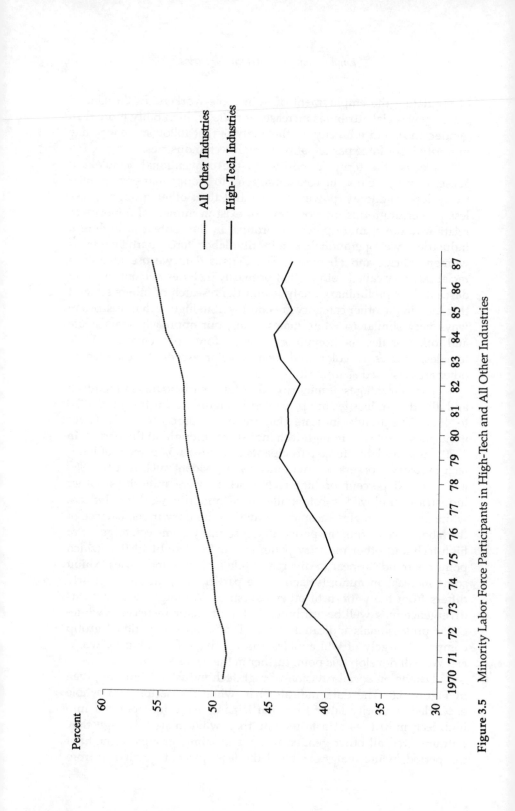

Figure 3.5 Minority Labor Force Participants in High-Tech and All Other Industries

Millions of Workers

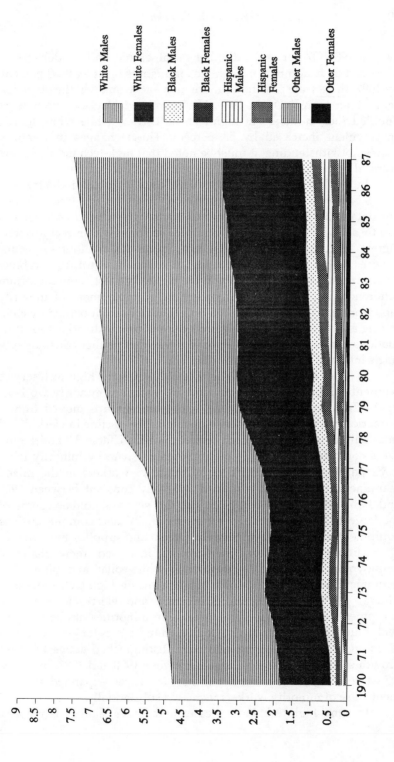

Figure 3.6   Race, Gender, and Ethnicity of Workers in High-Tech Industries

1970 to 1987 (37 percent). All other racial, ethnic, and gender groups increased their numbers in high-tech industries by at least 50 percent. By 1987, there were nine times more men and women in the other category than there were in 1970. Hispanics and blacks of both sexes doubled their numbers in high-tech industries, while white female employment increased by 58 percent. These changes in minority shares notwithstanding, it must be noted that high-tech industries are atypical in the continuing overrepresentation of white males.

In the last section, we introduced four high-tech industry segments based on specific occupational compositions and trends. While our data make it difficult to focus on each high-tech industry, we can use these high-tech segments to introduce some within-sector detail. Figure 3.7 contains percent minority figures for the four segments: services, white-collar manufacturing, mixed manufacturing, and blue-collar manufacturing. The data in the figure suggest some important differences among high-tech industries in employment of minority labor force participants. The data points have been smoothed by computing a moving average. This procedure allows us to adjust for fluctuations caused by sampling error in a way that neither adds nor subtracts information from the raw data.[8]

In sharp contrast to other service industries, the high-tech service segment exhibits a decline over time in percent of minority workers. By 1987, minority gender, racial, and ethnic groups moved from a numerical majority to a minority position. The decline in clerical and sales employment in high-tech services noted in Table 3.2 and Figure 3.4 is coincident with a loss of employment share by minority labor force participants. Participation by minority workers in the mixed manufacturing segment remained relatively constant between 1970 and 1987. This is noteworthy because this segment contains some of the largest U.S. high-tech industries: radio, TV, and communications equipment, electrical machinery, equipment and supplies, and aircraft.

Minority labor force participants increased their share of employment in two of the segments: white-collar and blue-collar manufacturing. The white-collar manufacturing high-tech industries (drugs, guided missiles and spacecraft, and electronic computer equipment) exhibit a collective increase in minorities of about 5 percent. Blue-collar manufacturing high-tech industries (engines and turbines and scientific instruments) were distinguished above for their growth in low-level blue-collar jobs between 1970 and 1987. In Figure 3.7 we see that, as the lower tier of these industries expanded, the segment's use of minority workers increased substantially.

In sum, high-tech industries exhibit larger shares of minority

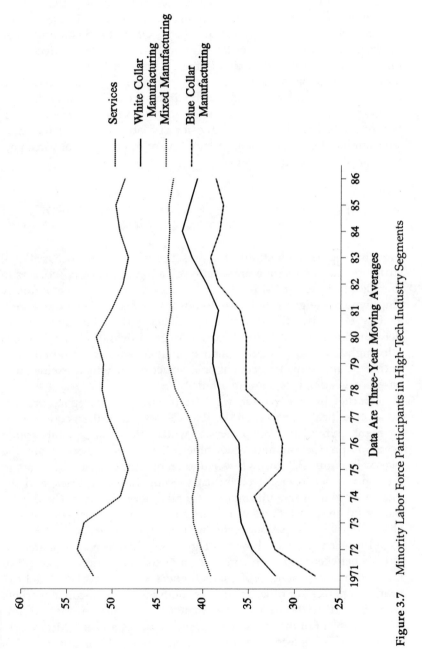

Figure 3.7 Minority Labor Force Participants in High-Tech Industry Segments

labor force participants by 1987. These increased shares notwithstanding, white and other males continue to constitute numerical majorities within the high-technology sector. These aggregate trends mask key differences, however, within the high-tech sector. While a decline in minority labor force participation is evident in service high-tech industries, proportional increases are found among white-collar and especially blue-collar manufacturing industries. This latter finding suggests that more insight can be gained by examining the intersection of the technical and social divisions of labor. In the next section, we examine the occupational distribution of minority labor force participants in high-tech industries.

THE INTERSECTION OF THE HIGH-TECH TECHNICAL AND SOCIAL DIVISIONS OF LABOR

Thus far, we have illustrated the presence of a two-tier occupational structure and the relative underrepresentation of minority workers in the high-tech sector. Much of the literature on high-tech industry employment suggests that these trends are associated with one another. That is, the two-tier structure—particularly the white-collar upper tier—amounts to a structural barrier for the integration of minorities into high-tech work. In the analysis that follows, we evaluate this notion of an exclusive occupational structure in which exclusion is based on gender, race, and/or ethnicity.

Earlier in this chapter, we introduced a four-category occupational classification based on the 1980 Census occupation codes: management, administrative, professional, technical; other white-collar; precision production; and, other blue-collar. These categories are displayed in Figure 3.8 for high-tech and all other industries. The bars in the figure refer to high-tech industry occupation categories, and the lines refer to the same information for all other industries. The data in the figure are percentages of minority labor force participants associated with each occupational category from 1970 to 1987.

In the early years shown in Figure 3.8, there is a very sharp difference between high-tech and other industries in terms of percent of minority management, professional, and technical workers. In 1970, nearly 35 percent of other industries' high-level, white-collar workers were minority labor force participants. Minorities constituted less than 15 percent of the management, professional, and technical workers in the 1970 high-tech sector. Some narrowing of this differential is evident until about 1984 when the gap between high-tech and other

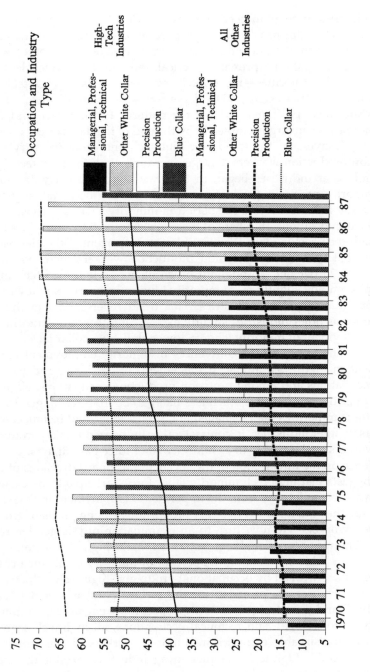

Figure 3.8 Minority Labor Force Participants in High-Tech and All Other Industries by Occupation Group

industries appears to become constant. Clearly, the upper tier of the high-tech sector has a smaller proportion of gender, racial, and ethnic minorities than other industries. Sectoral differences in other white-collar occupations (primarily clerical and sales) are much less pronounced. Minorities—most likely, women—in both high-tech and other industries occupy 60 to 65 percent of these middle-level, clerical white-collar positions. Indeed, the patterns for high-tech and other industries converge completely by the end of the data series.

Conversely, the trends for high-tech and other industry precision production workers diverge over time. Both the high-tech sector and other industries began in 1970 with approximately 15 percent minority precision production workers. While both industry types exhibit increases across the period in minority share of precision production positions, the share of these jobs occupied by minorities in the high-tech sector more than doubles to 37 percent. Other industries' percent of minority precision production workers increases to just under 25 percent. Throughout much of the period, high-tech industries employ slightly more minority blue-collar workers in lower-skill jobs than do other industries. This trend reverses late in the data series as other industries slightly exceed high-tech industries in their employment of minority labor in lower-skill, blue-collar jobs.

The most striking differences in minority employment are evident in Figure 3.8 among management, professional, and technical occupations and among precision production occupations. High-tech upper-tier workers are much less likely to be from racial, gender, and ethnic minorities than management, professional, and technical workers in other industries. In contrast, other industry precision production workers are less likely to be minority labor force participants. This evidence on the intersection of the social and technical divisions of labor suggests that high-tech minority labor force participants are excluded in a substantial way from the upper tier of employment in that sector. And, they are included in larger proportions among precision production workers. We now turn to an examination of this gender, racial, and ethnic occupational segregation *within* the high-tech sector.

In Table 3.3, data on the percent of minority labor force participants are arrayed by occupational group and high-tech industry segment. Figures are provided for the earliest point in our data series (1970) and the latest (1987). With respect to management, administrative, professional, and technical occupations, all high-tech segments evidence sizeable increases in minority workers in this upper tier. White-collar high-tech manufacturing industries exhibit the largest gain of minority workers. There is a similar increase in the upper tier held by minority labor force participants in blue-collar manufacturing industries. The percentage increase of minorities in high-tech service and mixed manufacturing industries is roughly half that of white-collar and blue-collar high-tech segments. Thus, though we have demonstrated that the upper-tier of the high-tech industry occupation structure is still largely the domain of white males, minority labor force participants have gained a larger share of employment in the high-tech industries we describe as white-collar manufacturing (drugs, missiles, and computers) and blue-collar manufacturing (engines and scientific instruments). The latter high-tech industry segment is very small, and hence, the percentage change does not represent a large number of jobs available for minorities. The white-collar manufacturing segment is a large expanding set of industries. This segment appears to be one source of upper-tier opportunities for minority labor force participants. It is important to note, however, that the fastest growing segment of the high-tech sector—services—exhibits the smallest percentage increase in minority employment in managerial, professional, and technical positions.

Table 3.3   Percent of Minority Labor Force Participants in High-Tech Industry Segments by Occupation Group and Year

Industry Segment	Administration, Management, Professional and Technical		Other White-Collar		Precision Prod.		Other Blue-Collar	
	1970	1987	1970	1987	1970	1987	1970	1987
Services	29.6	38.0	77.6	72.8	0.0	22.0	32.1	44.4
White-Collar Manufacturing	8.6	30.6	52.8	64.6	11.5	24.6	50.2	63.6
Mixed Manufacturing	10.3	20.9	55.9	69.5	15.0	43.8	55.8	55.9
Blue-Collar Manufacturing	12.8	35.4	52.0	53.0	10.6	19.0	26.6	49.2

Table 3.3 also details changes in minority representation in other white-collar (clerical and sales) occupations. The data for service high-tech industries appear to confirm our earlier suspicions that, as other white-collar jobs are eliminated in these industries, minority

labor force participation decreases. New word processing and data base management technologies introduced between 1970 and 1987 no doubt lessened the need for clerical support in these service industries where the products are often analytical and written. Two of the remaining high-tech segments exhibit increases on the order of 14 percent in other white-collar minority employment. Both high-tech white-collar manufacturing industries and mixed manufacturing industries exhibit an increment of this magnitude in minority labor force participants' share of clerical and sales jobs. The minority share of other white-collar occupations in high-tech blue-collar industries remains roughly the same across the period.

By definition, there are very few precision production occupations in the high-tech service segment. Thus, the data for such jobs in Table 3.3 should be interpreted with caution. By contrast, precision production is a relatively important component of white-collar manufacturing industries. Between 1970 and 1987, a 13 percent increase in minority labor participation in precision production is apparent in white-collar manufacturing industries. The largest increase in minority share to be found in Table 3.3 (29 percent) is indicated for precision production employment in mixed high-tech industries. This increase is important not only because of the magnitude but because the mixed high-tech industry segment is by far the largest of the four industry groups. Yet, considering the doubling of precision production jobs in this sector from 1970 to 1987, the growth of minority labor force participation seems rather modest. Though opportunities for minorities in these better production jobs are apparent, it nonetheless appears that nonminority workers continue to hold a disproportionate share of precision production jobs in the largest high-tech industry segment. Lastly, among blue-collar manufacturing industries, minority labor force participation in high-skilled, blue-collar jobs was up only 8 percent from 1970 to 1987.

The final occupational category listed on Table 3.3 is other blue collar. As Figure 3.3 indicates, this is an occupational group that declined dramatically from 1970 to 1987 in proportion to other occupational groups among high-tech industries. We interpret this aggregate decline in high-tech blue-collar work as a strong indication of production regimes based on static flexibility. These assembly and other manual jobs have likely been outsourced and/or automated to reduce the extent to which labor cost is a factor in production. In view of this loss of U.S. jobs, a static perspective on flexible production would suggest the need to maximize the flexibility of any remaining domestic blue-collar production labor.

One way to ensure labor flexibility is to employ vulnerable minority labor force participants. The data for other blue-collar employment in Table 3.3 suggest that this is precisely what has occurred in the high-tech sector. In a period of rapidly declining high-tech blue-collar employment opportunities, the minority shares of these jobs have remained constant or increased in all high-tech industry segments. The high-tech service and white-collar manufacturing industry segments exhibit a 12 percent increase in minority other blue-collar employment. Though lower-skill blue-collar employment declined by one-third within the large mixed high-tech industry segment, the share of those jobs held by minority labor force participants held constant at just over 50 percent. Finally, the percent change in other blue-collar employment in the blue-collar manufacturing industry segment is the second largest increase contained in Table 3.3. From 1970 to 1987, the minority share of blue-collar jobs increased by more than 20 percent. If a large representation of minority labor force participants makes for a flexible labor force, the high-tech sector's blue-collar production labor force is as flexible as any other major industrial sector.

TECHNICAL AND SOCIAL DIVISIONS IN PERSPECTIVE

Our interest in divisions of high-tech industry labor has led us to examine the technical (occupational or task) and social (race, gender, and/or ethnic) dimensions. Employing data on high-tech industries from 1970 to 1987, we describe this critical period of development for the technology sector. Consistent with the findings of others, we have noted that high-tech industries are indeed expanding and creating new employment opportunities. Because of the small aggregate size of the high-tech sector, however, these new opportunities are not great in number.

When we look within what we and many others typically treat as the high-tech sector, we find substantial heterogeneity in patterns of growth, distributions of occupations, and concentrations of minority labor force participants. This sectoral heterogeneity notwithstanding, our account of the high-tech industries in the aggregate details a balkanized two-tier technical division of labor and a restrictive social division of labor that admits minority labor force participants in lower proportions than other industries. When we examine the intersection of these technical and social dimensions, we find relatively few minorities in the upper tier of the high-tech industry occupational structure. We also observe minority labor force participants deployed in blue-collar production jobs in a manner that enhances the static flexibility of high-tech production labor.

In the second chapter, we discussed dynamic flexibility as an alternative to static flexibility. If there were a U.S. industrial sector that could accommodate dynamic production strategies, surely it is high technology. Yet, the analysis of the technical and social divisions of labor in this chapter suggest that the regime of static flexibility is as dominant in the high-tech sector as it is in other industries. It is still possible that high-tech industries' spatial division of labor reflects dynamic flexibility. The high-tech spatial division of labor is the subject of analysis in the following chapter.

Chapter Four

High-Tech Industrial Development
and the Spatial Division of Labor

In this chapter, we address the spatial division of labor generated by high-tech industrial development. First, we discuss the various rationales given for the development of high-tech industries. Some of these explanations are national in character and are based on concerns for U.S. economic development and national security. Other explanations are linked to the intense competition among states, regions, and locales for new industry. Second, we discuss theories of firm location with particular emphasis on the theories relevant for the geographical distribution of high-tech industries. Finally, we employ Census data to examine the spatial division of high-tech labor.

The well-documented crisis in the U.S. economic system has raised concerns about the role of maturing industries in the maintenance of U.S. standing in the global marketplace. One popular response to this dilemma is to focus on the development of high-growth "sunrise" industries that are viewed as strategic for the maintenance of national economic and military security. For reasons discussed below, the high-tech sector is often considered a key player in the resolution of what some view as the coming U.S. industrial crisis.

WHY HIGH TECHNOLOGY?

Drawing on economic theorists such as Joseph Schumpeter, many view technological innovation as a prime impetus in the process of capitalist economic growth.[1] Schumpeter describes this process as a series of technological explosions in which innovations lead to invest-

69

ment and economic expansion. As competition increases, production costs rise and markets become saturated. Then, new technological advances initiate subsequent waves of economic growth. While some industries and product groups necessarily decline, new industries and products will sustain economic growth. Following this line of reasoning, policymakers view industries on the cutting edge of innovation as leaders in the revitalization of the U.S. economy. These industries are thought to have potential for enormous positive influence on the general economic climate. High-tech industry expansion is expected to generate direct and indirect gains in employment and market demand.

The leading role of the high-tech sector is epitomized by the semiconductor industry which, as Wilson and co-workers have noted, has initiated its own series of innovative cycles.[2] As transistor technology was approaching maturity in the 1960s, bipolar integrated logic circuits were introduced. As this technology matured, advances in metal oxide semiconductor technology enabled major breakthroughs in microprocessors and electronic memory. Over time, the end uses of semiconductors have expanded through these cycles to include radios, televisions, calculators, computers, automobiles, and a host of other mass market and specialty items.

Through interrelationships with other sectors, the influence of technological innovations is diffused throughout the economy. The emergence of textile processing machines, for example, ultimately facilitated the use of synthetic fibers. Similarly, advances in metallurgy allowed for the development of the jet engine, and machine tooling methods promoted the use of alloy steels.[3] A study by Townsend and colleagues found that innovations in one industrial sector averaged close to ten other sector applications.[4] According to their findings, high-tech innovations in instruments were applied in forty-four other sectors, electronic capital goods resulted in twenty-three other sector applications, and electronic components generated eighteen. This ability to affect other sectors is an important reason why high-tech industries are attractive to economic planners and policymakers.

While new products and production techniques do serve as an impetus for developments in other sectors, the effects of high-tech industries on employment are less conclusive. The research by Riche and co-workers cited in chapter 3 reports that employment in high-tech industries increased significantly faster than all wage and salaried employment between 1972 and 1982. However, total employment in these industries varied from 4.7 to 15.3 percent of the total labor force, depending on how broadly the high-tech sector is defined.[5] Using a rather narrow definition of high-tech industries, our analysis in the previous chapter suggests that these industries are not likely now or in the near future to employ a large share of the U.S. labor force. And, some high-tech industries employ fewer domestic workers now than they did a few years ago.

Moreover, technical innovations that have altered industrial and occupational structures have not necessarily generated overall employment growth. Allan and Timothy Hunt project that, while the robotics industry will create between 32,000 and 64,000 jobs by 1990, robots will also displace between 100,000 and 200,000 workers in this time period.[6] Not just a function of automation, job displacement also occurs when older products such as electronic vacuum tubes are replaced by newer ones such as semiconductors. Weiss reports that the American economy is likely to lose 25 million jobs by the year 2000 due to the introduction of new technologies.[7]

A further concern is that structural unemployment created by the decline of traditional key industries will not be alleviated by high-tech industrialization.[8] Displaced steel workers are not likely to have the skills required for technical jobs in the desirable upper tier of the high-tech occupational structure. Alternative low-skill production and service jobs will result in lower wages and a decline in the standard of living of these workers.

In a larger context, a final consideration is that high-tech industries may be more a consequence than a cause of economic growth. Richard Nelson suggests that advances in education in both the United States and Japan preceded high-tech industrialization and that the newest leaders in the international marketplace exhibit advanced development in all sectors. High technology is only a small part of the total economic output of core nations. In terms of the strategic importance of high tech for national dominance, Nelson also notes that technical information is transferred so widely and rapidly that national boundaries have become meaningless.[9]

We conclude that while the high-tech sector has exhibited growth in employment and the potential for great impact upon other industries, it has yet to provide a solution for the increasing problems of unemployment and underemployment that are generated by a shifting economic base. In the sections below, it will become obvious that our pessimism is not shared by the development community and state policymakers. First, we review the confusion surrounding national high-tech policy. Then, we turn to strategies employed at the state and local levels to promote high-tech development.

NATIONAL HIGH-TECH POLICIES AND CONCERNS

While researchers debate high technology as a development strategy, the idea continues to have widespread appeal to economic planners and policymakers at national, regional, and local levels. Unlike our Japanese rivals, however, domestic policies for high-tech development are not coherent or consistent and are best described as "de facto." Typically, the policies call for support of education- and government-related research and development through such agencies as the Departments of Defense and Agriculture, NASA, and the National Science Foundation. To be sure, these policies for high-tech development have proved successful in certain specific product markets. The United States continues to be the largest producer and exporter of civil aircraft, computers, and semiconductors. And in some critical areas of technological innovation, such as artificial intelligence, supercomputers, and superconductivity, U.S. companies are also considered dominant.

Yet, the intense concentration of research and development in defense-related organizations raises concerns on the part of many. Expenditures by the military constitute more than 70 percent of the total research and development budget of the government. Harrison and Bluestone note:

> Almost the entire development (perhaps 70 to 80 percent) of such 'cutting-edge' technologies as lasers, artificial intelligence, fuel-efficient jumbo jet engines, superspeed computers, high-density semiconductors, vision-equipped robots, computer-aided manufacturing systems, and advanced synthetic materials is now controlled by military policy. A new Pentagon office is expected to account, by 1990, for a full fifth of the nation's high-technology venture capital. And none of these statistics include President Reagan's Strategic Defense Initiative (SDI) which, according to plan, would eventually enroll more scientists and engineers than either the Apollo space program or the development of the atomic bomb.[10]

Concerns about the domination of innovation by the military have been voiced by academicians, business representatives, and even those working in the defense industries. Current defense research involving the use of laser, fiber optics, and sensor technologies may have other applications, but security constraints limit the diffusion of this knowledge to commercial sectors. Much of the knowledge gained in this type of research remains inaccessible for years, and frequently, the documentation is destroyed. Consequently, the commercial sector must retrace research and innovation steps already taken by the military to attain this knowledge. This amounts to a very inefficient and lengthy reinventing of a high-tech wheel.

There are concerns that international transfers of technology, occurring in many of the United State's dominant industries, may also threaten the nation's long-run economic potential. A controversial joint venture between Japanese companies manufacturing aircraft parts and Boeing, for example, permits the training of Japanese engineers in the design and production of aircraft. With this knowledge, Japan hopes to produce its own aircraft to compete with U.S. industry in a few years. The Reagan and Bush administrations recently sanctioned an agreement between the Japanese and General Dynamics that will facilitate the Japanese production of the new FSX jet fighter. Instead of conventional F-16 fighter planes, the U.S. will sell the technology to build a new generation of aircraft. The long-range orientation of the Japanese is apparent in these examples of technology transfer. This forward-looking posture assumed by Japan and a number of Western European countries suggests that the international high-tech marketplace is changing in an important, qualitative way. The short-range orientation of American policy may well endanger its future stake in global high-tech markets.

Critics argue, then, that U.S. economic security is at risk through international technology transfers and joint ventures. But, they also contend that our national security may be at risk as well. Many are alarmed that U.S. defense systems are constructed with high-tech parts produced by international competitors. A 1989 *Newsweek* report quotes MIT researcher Michael Chinworth, "If you knew how many foreign chips are in the F-16 and other advanced weapons, you would be terrified."[11] The high-tech market is an international market. The division of the production process among national entities is just as apparent in these industries as it has been for years in mature manufacturing industries. The difference lies in the critical role high-tech industries play in our national and economic security.

In sum, while de facto national policies concerning high-tech development have produced some successes, they may also threaten U.S. economic and national security. The continued U.S. dominance of certain high-tech arenas is being challenged by foreign competitors. And domestic technological advances are occasionally compromised by companies seeking short-run economic gains at the expense of long-run economic stability for the nation as a whole. As we move into the twenty-first century, it is certainly questionable whether a haphazard approach to high-tech policies continues to be in the best interest of the United States.

The incoherence of national high-tech policy does not dampen the enthusiasm for high-tech development at regional, state, and local levels. Growth centers such as Austin, Dallas, Denver, and San Diego have emerged where defense-related high-tech industries concentrate and eventually influence an entire region. From the beginning of the product cycle, effects reverberate throughout an area, resulting in innovative spinoff firms. As industries mature, branch plants using standardized manufacturing processes appear. Federal funds are often used to provide infrastructure necessities demanded by high-tech firms, making the companies even more attractive to state, regional, and local representatives.

Various strategies to attract high-tech industries are implemented by public officials, private citizens, and interest groups. At the regional level, multistate advocacy groups attempt to frame development. A recent report from the Southern Growth Policies Board, for example, outlines its recommendations for the economic development of the region in the 1990s. The report stresses the need for upgrading education at all levels to provide a skilled labor force for tomorrow's high-tech jobs. Technological innovation within the region is to be generated by centers of excellence at several research universities, enhanced graduate programs in science and engineering, joint university/private-sector commercialization of innovations, and funding for "the technological research which sparks the economy."[12]

At the state level, an eclectic assortment of strategies is used to sell a state's abundant resources to potential high-tech employers. In Alabama, Governors Wallace and Hunt have traveled extensively to Japan and Korea to discuss business opportunities in Alabama. Industrial revenue bonds are sold by the state to finance construction of business facilities which remain tax-free until the bonds are retired. Training facilities like the Alabama Center for Advanced Technology Transfer are state-subsidized to provide technically trained workers for specific companies like Boeing, General Electric, and Intergraph located in northern Alabama. Marketing consultants are hired by the state to advertise the business potential of Alabama on billboards and in national high-tech and finance magazines. Legal inducements like tort reform legislation have been cited as added attractions for high-tech and other firms to locate in the state. Indeed, Alabama's legislation has been touted a model for other states to follow.[13]

Alabama is not alone in its efforts to attract high-tech industries. The National Governors Association reports that task forces to promote states' technological growth exist in 27 states. Thirty-three states have customized job training centers to provide workers for current or incoming firms. Many states are also developing programs for upgrading higher education and strengthening its role in economic development.[14]

Similarly, local communities believe there is much to be gained by attracting high-tech industries. While local developers may not be aware of theories of technology and economic expansion, they view high-tech industries as clean, stable, capital-intensive, high-wage, and able to attract well-educated, affluent employees. Local officials argue that high-tech firms create jobs directly and indirectly through an expanded sector of business services that caters to the needs of high-tech firms.

In many areas, the local chamber of commerce plays a leading role in marketing the community to high-tech industry. Chamber representatives, city officials, and private delegates from local banks, the media, and utilities make several trips yearly to recruit new industry. Local firms are also active in shaping their community's high-tech landscape. In Huntsville, Alabama, the chamber's major source for identifying prospective firms is the advice and recommendations of existing high-tech firms in the area.[15] While this approach may inhibit competition, this strategy is a decided advantage for local employers who can influence the development of the area labor market.

A major incentive employed at the local level to attract high-tech industries is the building of publicly financed, technology-oriented research parks. In Huntsville and elsewhere, research parks seek high-tech firms offering proximity to transportation, markets, and factor inputs. The clustering of several companies in a single area like a park is also deemed desirable by technical professionals. As discussed in chapter 2, upper-tier high-tech workers enjoy access to external as well as internal labor markets. Engineers and other professional and technical high-tech employees frequently work for one company until a particular contract or project is completed and then move on to a neighboring firm offering new challenges and better opportunities.[16]

Luger and Goldstein argue that the success of Stanford Research Park and Research Trangle Park has inspired areas across the country to establish research parks. They report a national 300 percent increase in the number of research parks since 1982.[17] These researchers caution that, while some of these parks may succeed in becoming viable centers for high-tech development, many will not succeed. In Edward Bee's words, "Courting high-tech industry is not a quick marriage for most developers." Unlike mature American industries, high-tech companies demand more than just cheap labor. They demand technically trained and skilled workers, research universities, high-quality business and transportation services (including airlines), and an enticing quality of life that hinges on good schools, recreation, housing, and health care. A research park in an area without these kinds of attributes is highly unlikely to survive.[18]

As some regional, state, and local strategies for attracting and retaining high-tech industries succeed and others fail, an uneven development of the high-tech sector has emerged. This results in a spatial division of labor among high-tech industries that has been recognized by previous research and is examined further below. By understanding the process that produces the geographic patterns of high-tech industries, both policymakers and developers can make more informed decisions concerning the role of high-tech industries in local, regional and national economies. In the next section we will discuss several approaches for understanding and interpreting the spatial division of labor.

LOCATION THEORIES AND THE HIGH-TECH
SPATIAL DIVISION OF LABOR

In this section, we explicate three theories of industrial location, noting their relevance for understanding the location of high-tech industries and citing supporting empirical research. Two explanations derive from familiar orientations: neoclassical and radical theories. A third explanation is grounded in recent work on industrial restructuring. The neoclassical economic theory of firm location is implicit, if not explicit, in most strategies used by industrial developers for attracting high-tech industries.

Neoclassical Economic Approaches

Among neoclassical economists, location theory reduces the development process to the sum of individual firm-level decisions that attempt to minimize costs and maximize revenues. When sites are considered for the location of business establishments, the input factors of production (land, labor, raw materials, and and capital) and other geographic considerations (proximity to markets, transportation, time, and costs) are weighed. The particular mix of these factors is then evaluated in terms of costs and revenue potentials, and the most advantageous site is chosen. Economic theories of development emphasize the agglomeration process in which these environmental attractions lead to growth centers where commodity linkages and access to larger markets allow for the attainment of certain economies of scale in production.[19]

The product life cycle approach is a variant of the neoclassical approach in which decentralization is posited to occur as the production process matures and the required skill level of workers declines. Over the life cycle of a product, production facilities can move away from the costly center to economical peripheral sites. While this approach has been used extensively to explain the spatial configurations of high-tech industries, it is not without its critics.[20] Walker, for example argues that product life cycle and agglomeration approaches are limited in accounting for many of the location decisions evidenced by firms in particular industries.[21] While each approach has some utility in certain cases, the conditions under which the explanations hold must be carefully specified.

A common theme in neoclassical approaches is that differences in types and rates of growth across areas can ultimately be reduced to natural differences in factors of production, proximity to markets, and present industrial mixes of an area. Firms make rational location decisions based on these criteria. Because of differential natural endowments across areas, tendencies toward agglomeration, and different stages in the product life cycle, unevenness in the development process is bound to occur. Some areas will become centers for research, development, and product incubation. Others will exhibit concentrations of mass production facilities. Still other areas may have no industry at all. Yet, neoclassical theorists maintain that the consequences of uneven development are only temporary imperfections. Ultimately, a tendency toward equilibrium will reduce disparities across areas.

Studies of high-tech industrial location in the neoclassical tradition typically ask high-tech managers to identify factors that are most important in site location decisions. Researchers generate frequency distributions that rank order these factors in terms of importance in location determination. A study reported in *Electronic Business*, for example, ranked the following factors from highest to lowest: skilled labor force, favorable labor relations, financial aid and other incentives, transportation and communications, low wage levels, access to foreign markets, suitable real estate, large domestic market, clean environment, research and development facilities, and training facilities.[22] Another study of high-tech location by economist Chris Paul finds, "The major input into the creation or production of high technology on all levels is professionally trained research personnel. Where these individuals are readily available, high technology may...flourish ...[where] there exists no such concentration of research technicians and scientists any proposition to establish a viable concentration of high-technology industries...is unlikely to succeed."[23] While many factors are cited as important, this type of location research has emphasized the salience of a highly skilled, specialized labor force as a primary factor in determining the geography of high-tech industries.

Radical Approaches

The strongest criticisms of neoclassical economic theories of location come from the left, particularly Marxist theorists, some of whom interpret location decisions solely in terms of the social relations of production. Exemplifying this perspective, Richard Peet states, "The terms popularly used to rationalize the relocation of United States manufacturing industry as a move from the Frostbelt to Sunbelt (implying locational determination by natural relations of production) represent an ideological diversion from a more essential truth."[24] This truth is the notion that "natural resources are used, and space arranged and rearranged, under the control of the social relations of production of a capitalist economy."[25]

The Marxist approach attributes the spatial diversification of manufacturing industries to contradictory forces of equalization and differentiation that characterize capitalism.[26] Equalizing tendencies are seen as the capitalist mode of production supercedes other modes, proletarianization increases, and technology advances, resulting in increased concentration and centralization of capital. Differentiation results from the division of labor and capital along dimensions labeled "general" (industry versus agriculture), "particular" (type of industry), "individual capitalist" (idiosyncratic), and "detailed" (occupational). Equalization and differentiation result in cyclical, uneven geographic development along regional, sectoral, and organizational lines.

Cycles occur as the result of crises of overproduction and falling profit rates that regularly occur in capitalist systems where productive capital becomes obsolete and devalued. Similar to Schumpeter, Mandel argues that, when a crisis occurs, new technologies are adopted that can result in the generation of new particular divisions (industrial sectors). Capital flows from less profitable sectors to new ones which expand rapidly.[27] These new investments, facilitated by the credit system and the state, tend to generate new geographic patterns. As Smith states:

> Insofar as sectors of the economy are spatially centralized, then, the place-specific character of devaluation translates sectoral crises directly into geographical crises affecting entire regions. The obsolescence of old technologies and the rise of new ones, so vital to capitalism, is simultaneously the transformation of old spatial structures into new ones.[28]

The radical perspective suggests that innovative high-tech industries should exhibit spatial configurations that differ from those of more mature industries.

Restructuring Theories

Storper and Walker explicate what we refer to as a "restructuring" approach that draws on both the neoclassical and radical perspectives.[29] Their major criticism of neoclassical economics location theory is its "treatment of labor as just another 'factor of production' of little importance to location outside of a few labor-intensive industries." As restructuring theorists outline their own more complex and dynamic theoretical approach to understanding the spatial division of labor, they attempt to "push the 'labor factor' to the forefront in the analysis of the modern geography of industrial capitalism."[30] Unlike radical theorists, restructuring proponents do not see labor as an undifferentiated mass completely subject to capitalist exploitation. The spatial division of labor results from complex capital and labor processes and power relationships that are shaped by both natural and social constraints.

Restructuring theories hold that factors of production specific to particular areas have diminished in importance for understanding the location of industrial establishments. This claim is based on technological progress in communications and transportation, the emergence of new markets, automation that allows separation of production stages, synthetic materials that reduce reliance on geographically dispensed raw materials, and the power of large corporations to shape and direct production and circulation in previously underdeveloped sites. Because it is variable, labor remains an important and unique factor of production unlike all other commodities. The dimensions along which labor varies (conditions of purchase, performance capacity, actual performance, and conditions for its reproduction) form the basis of geographic variation within industries.[31] Thus, while radical location theorists view labor solely in terms of its costs, restructuring theorists identify several dimensions of labor that can be important for location and spatial distribution.

Demand for labor, the cornerstone of locational decision-making, is shaped by certain constraints set by the nature of the product sector, the firm, and the power of the capitalist. Both labor and capital have bargaining power. As they are mutually interdependent, worker power will be diminished or enhanced by the nature of the product, its market structure, the organization of the production process (craft, continuous process, or mechanized or manual assembly), and the availability of other jobs (labor market structure). Employers will also be limited by the product, perceived imperatives for the organization of the production process, and pressures generated by oligopolistic or competitive product market structures. Thus, the bargaining powers of both labor and capital vary among industries, across locations, and over time. Spatial divisions of labor, then, are in a constant state of change as bargaining power varies within these dynamic constraints.

While the importance of technology in this perspective is particularly applicable to high-tech industries, the restructuring model is not one of technological determinism. While new technologies might bring about development in new industrial sectors, "technology is also a means of class struggle between capital and labor."[32] Thus, labor and capital may use technology as a bargaining chip or control strategy to further interests. Managers may employ specialized machinery to produce a more complex and deskilled division of labor that is easily replaced and, hence, controlled. Labor unions may resist job-eliminating automation or accept technology with assurances of job security.

Most importantly, similar technologies can be used in different ways. The choice of static or dynamic uses of technology, for example, reflect very different social relations and have different implications for further innovation. While static flexibility tends to restrict advancements, dynamic flexibility is more encouraging of continuous innovation. And, as suggested above, the development of new technologies within the national defense context may diminish diffusion of innovations that might flourish as commercial developments in the private sector. In these ways, power relationships that govern the control and use of technology regulate the extent of diffusion or progression of technical innovation.

A unique and important contribution of the restructuring approach elaborated by Storper is the notion that area restructuring is a reciprocal process.[33] As industries are attracted to areas for reasons outlined above, industries also shape the areas in which they locate. Industries create the type of location that will enhance profitability. On observing the location strategies of various high-tech industries, Storper reasons:

> New industries seem to form their initial production complexes in relatively undeveloped (though not underdeveloped) regions without deep (or at least without similar) industrial histories.... Industries producing new use-values or radically new processes have their own locational requirements that are unlike those of previously existing industries...these new industries must have some way of attracting the factors of production they need, thereby causing territorial production complexes to come into being in regions that did not previously possess those factors. It seems that new industries wield a kind of factor attraction power due to their high profit rates and consequent abilities to pay certain factors (the relatively expensive ones), in addition to taking advantage of the frequent slackness of allocation of relatively cheap factors in capitalist economies.[34]

Many high-tech industries in oligopolistic and competitive markets consist of large corporate enterprises that possess power to expand possibilities for site location. Venture capital, so important in these industries, tends to follow these large corporations, reducing risks associated with investment.[35] The location of a large high-tech corporation attracts other satellite firms and encourages the migration of certain types of skilled labor. And local labor is eventually generated through enhanced area educational and training facilities. As much as high-tech centers are based where factors of production are most favorable, they are also prime movers in the redesign of the local industrial landscape.

A final aspect of the restructuring approach is its concern for the larger macroeconomic context in which the process of uneven development occurs. The investment decisions that create the uneven development process are seen in the dynamic cycles and stages of capital accumulation. Storper writes:

Industrywide and worldwide dynamics are antecedent to factor-supply conditions in generating the impulses toward locational shifts in investments; firms do not move simply in response to factor-supply differentials that had, after all, existed for some time. These decisions are strongly geared to macroeconomic conditions: The corporate survivors of each crisis and merger wave in the economy are a new breed in terms of scale and organization. Their investments are bearers of new products and processes, whereas obsolete processes and uncompetitive plants and firms disappear. Industrial restructuring means alterations in product mix, production technique, and organizational structure. These events control factor demands and trigger spatial reorganization of production to secure them, and open up new opportunities to exploit preexisting factor supply differentials.[36]

In her analysis of the high-tech regional division of labor, Amy Glasmeier adopts a similar perspective, emphasizing the importance of labor in location decisions.[37] Like Storper and Walker, she notes several considerations involving labor. The first of these focuses on constraints of products and production technologies on labor requirements accorded to different stages of high-tech production. These constraints mean that research and development activities must be located near corporate headquarters to facilitate communication between technical, marketing, and financial sectors. Initial production of new products is also located near to these centers while the later stages of production, particularly standardized assembly, are located in domestic remote sites or even other countries.

A second labor consideration recognizes the different social relations of production that exist for different production stages. In high-tech industries, this is evident in strategies that separate technical workers from production workers. On the one hand, technical workers have more bargaining power because of firm-specific training and a high external demand for their labor. From the employer's perspective, technical workers must be provided with incentives to remain with the company. Retention inducements such as stock options, high levels of autonomy, and internal labor markets are made available to technical and professional employees. Production workers, on the other hand, are more easily replaced and consequently have limited bargaining power. Moreover, as discussed in chapter 2, high-tech industries require considerable flexibility to alter production processes and locations. This results in frequent hirings and layoffs of production workers. Centralization of production and technical development in one location (either a common building or even a common community) might encourage production workers to demand similar privileges and benefits accorded to technical personnel. Incentives that promote low turnover among upper-tier professional and technical workers might conflict with employers' strategies for lower-tier production workers. Indeed, this contingency approach to management was found in the organizational studies and our own interviews cited in the second chapter.

Glasmeier finds a separation of technical and professional workers and production workers between regions as well as a concentration of technical activities in regions and states with a spatial concentration of banking, corporate headquarters, and business services such as the Northeast and California. She also finds that high-tech industries require and seek a highly skilled labor force found near research universities with strong engineering programs and defense or space installations. She reiterates the importance of defense spending in the creation of a spatial division of labor in high-tech industries as 48 percent of the nation's aerospace engineers, 38 percent of the nation's physicists, and 18 percent of all mathematicians are employed in defense-related sectors. Finally, she notes that the spatial division of labor for high-tech industries has a geography that differs from that of the previous industrial era.

Theoretical Approaches in Perspective

While all three approaches suggest that high-tech industries have adopted their own unique spatial configuration, the restructuring perspective draws on the most useful aspects of the neoclassical and radical traditions. The restructuring viewpoint emphasizes that variations in high-tech development are linked to local differences in skill levels and industry differences in product stages. Moreover, skill levels and product stages must be understood in a larger framework of local management and labor relationships. The restructuring approach recognizes the dynamic and multidimensional nature of the demand for labor and how it shapes the nature of products, the organization of production, product and labor market structures, and the bargaining power accorded to labor and employers.

Based on the restructuring argument and empirical evidence, Castells reaches the following conclusions for understanding the location of high-tech industries and the resulting spatial division of labor which we find particularly useful:

1. Because of the nature of the product, high-tech industries are most likely located near major universities with a good supply of highly skilled, technically trained workers.

2. High-tech industries tend to cluster in established centers for space and defense activities, particularly test sites.

3. High-tech industries which require great flexibility and innovation tend to locate where anti-union sentiment is high. (The notion of flexibility used by Castells parallels the static flexibility concept discussed in previous chapters.)

4. High-tech industries tend to locate where available venture capital exists to finance more nontraditional manufacturing production.

5. Given the discrete nature of production for many high-tech industries, the activities of research and development, fabrication, assembly, and testing are separated spatially to take advantage of the different social relations of production that characterize these stages.[38]

We contend that this separation characterized by Castells reflects a static approach to the problems of flexibility.

Using different data and methods than those of previous studies, we assess these conclusions to the extent that our data permit. Like most studies on high-tech industry location, our analysis uses data on workers, not on firms. It is assumed that the location and distribution of workers reflects high-tech firms' decision-making patterns. This analysis seeks to identify the spatial location patterns of high-tech industries and the spatial divisions of labor within this sector along industry and occupational lines. Further, we will compare these patterns to those for more mature industries, trying to ascertain distinctive geographic characteristics of the high-tech industrial sector.

WHERE HIGH-TECH CENTERS ARE LOCATED

Previous research on the high-technology spatial division of labor has either focused on well-known urban high-tech centers such as Silicon Valley or Boston or on entire states.[39] Both approaches are problematic. The former ignores the more common or prevalent forms of high-tech industrialization that occur outside well-known centers.[40] The latter method ignores the wide variation in high-tech industrialization

within states. High-tech centers are not statewide, but local labor markets within states or, as we find below, labor markets that cross state
lines. In the analysis that follows, we employ a 1 percent 1980 Census
Public Use Microdata Sample D (PUMS-D) that delineates local labor
market areas based on journey-to-work patterns.[41] From the Census
data, we have identified three local labor markets in four regions of
the United States that have the highest percentages of full-time labor
force participants employed in high-tech industries. We consider
these labor market areas to be high-tech centers in that high-tech
industries provide salient employment opportunities in the local
labor market. This same measure has been called a "high-tech depen-
dency ratio" by Glasmeier and co-workers in their 1983 study of the
spatial tendencies of high-tech industries.[42] We focus on high-tech
centers because the intent is to identify the distinctive spatial
attributes of high-tech employment most apparent in areas most
dependent on this sector.

To be sure, the use of a percentage-based measure introduces
several biases into the identification of high-tech centers. Since standardized manufacturing firms typically employ more workers than
product development or research facilities, areas with large high-tech
production facilities are more likely to be represented.[43] Also, rural
areas with single dominant high-tech firms are more likely be identified as high-tech centers than are large urban areas in which many
high-tech workers compose smaller percentages of local labor forces.
Despite these biases, the high-tech centers we identify using this
methodology are the same ones noted in other studies. We believe
this approach produces the best indication of areas that have significant high-tech components in their local economy.

Previous research on high-tech firm location has relied on aggregate data like the Census of Manufacturing. PUMS-D allows us to
generate custom aggregate area profiles from data on individuals.
More importantly, the individual-level data allow us to assess the
socioeconomic implications for individual residents of a local high-
tech presence. Another advantage of PUMS-D, relative to other public
use census data, is that the D File permits identification of high-tech
centers in rural as well as urban areas. The location of high-tech production facilities in nonmetropolitan areas is not uncommon and corroborates our contention that limited bargaining power of rural workers is an attraction for firms engaged in high-tech standardized
production. Another advantage of these data is that the labor market
areas are defined as commuting nuclei. While major metropolitan
areas consist of multiple sets of commuting patterns, PUMS-D allows

us to focus specifically on high-tech workers' places of residence and employment when these enclaves are parts of larger urban centers.

Figure 4.1 depicts the locations of the high-tech labor market areas in four U.S. regions: West, Southeast, Midwest, and Northeast. Table 4.1 details characteristics of these labor market areas, including numbers of workers sampled and percent employed in high-tech industries. As the map indicates, while high-tech employment centers are identified in all regions of the United States, the percent of high-tech workers in these centers varies from 11 (Huntsville, Alabama) to 20 percent (Rochester, New York). The highest percentages of high-tech workers in these labor markets tend not be in the Southeast, where labor costs are lower, but in states with traditionally higher wages—California, New York, and Indiana. High-tech industries obviously do not necessarily adhere to the location trends of traditional industries that have exhibited a recent preference for Sunbelt locations.

The importance of military, space and/or university settings for growth in high-tech industries is seen in several of the high-tech centers identified in this study. Silicon Valley (near Stanford University), Los Alamos, New Mexico, and Huntsville, Alabama are all space or defense centers. High-tech centers in Vermont and New Hampshire, north of Boston and MIT suggest the importance of nearby established research centers to supply personnel and rapid communications for adjacent high-tech areas. The Boston labor market itself does not appear as a high-tech center because of its diversified industrial base. Labor markets adjacent to the larger areas undoubtedly contain spinoff firms and satellite industries that provide major high-tech employment opportunities.

A lack of union strength is noted by Castells and others as an incentive for high-tech industry locations requiring the greatest flexibility and innovation. This appears to hold for many of the high-tech centers identified in this study, but not for all. Low union membership (less than 15 percent) is characteristic of Vermont, New Hampshire, Tennessee, Virginia, Kansas, New Mexico, Texas, and Alabama.[44] On the other hand, 25 percent of the labor force is unionized in New York, Indiana, and California.[45]

Innovation aside, the presence of a flexible production labor force appears to be an important determinant of nonunion location. Most common among the high-tech centers identified in this analysis are industries in the later stages of production. As business cycles and market fluctuations exert pressures, these industries derive flexibility from adding or deleting workers. For example, petrochemicals; plas-

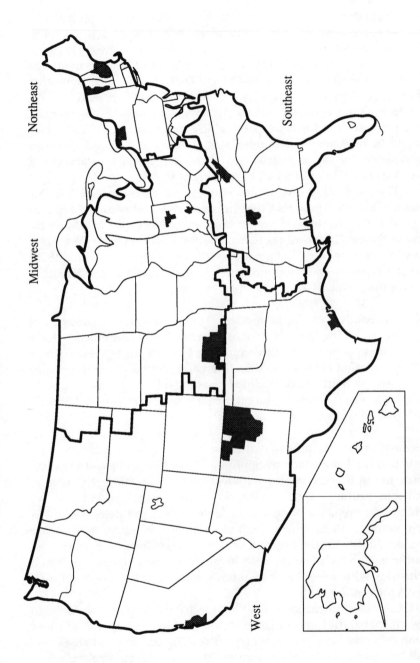

Northeast

Midwest

Southeast

West

Figure 4.1 U.S. High-Tech Labor Market Areas by Region

tics and synthetics; radio, TV, and communications equipment; photographic equipment; engines and turbines; aircraft and parts; and electrical machinery are for the most part mature industries. These are industries we identified in the last chapter as exhibiting occupational profiles suggestive of static flexibility. That is, there are signs that labor force sizes are manipulated to meet changes in demand. We should note, however, the center displaying highest employment in truly innovative industries (space vehicles, missiles, and parts) is also located in an extremely antiunion site: Huntsville, Alabama. A better explanation for the industrial mix there is proximity to army and NASA installations, not a lack of union power.

The availability of venture capital is not easily assessed in this research, but we know that the American financial sector is expanding out of its traditional concentrations in the Northeast and Midwest United States. Green argues that while the South and the West were slow to integrate into capital markets, the economic crisis of the 1970s and the types of emerging industries in these regions have begun to reverse this trend.[46] Green finds that, by 1983,

> the South had the largest amount of deposits in commercial banks among the four regions. The Northeast continued to have a larger proportion of the country's bank deposits, relative to its population. However, the differences between the Northeast and the South have declined considerably over this period. In both relative and absolute terms, the South's deficit in capital is disappearing.[47]

Regional economic shifts notwithstanding, Green's research also suggests that the loans made by Southern banks tend to be conservative. Thus, the opportunities for high-tech industrialization that require available venture capital in the South are increasing but still lag behind other regions. Note also in Table 4.1 that the percent of high-tech workers in Southern high-tech centers is lower than other regions. And, with the exception of the Huntsville labor market area, Southern high-tech employment involves well-established, high-tech industries with lower rates of innovation and, thus, lower requirements for venture capital.

Castells's conclusions about high-tech industrial location point to several spatial divisions of labor within the high-tech sector. The first along industry lines occurs when various regions or local areas specialize in particular high-tech industries in their development process. The second occurs when firms spatially separate technical and professional workers from lower skilled production workers using a contingency management approach—a sign of static flexibility. Using Census data from the high-tech centers identified here, we next examine industrial and occupational spatial divisions of labor across regions.

Table 4.1 High-Tech Centers, Workers, and Industries by U.S. Region

Region	Labor Market Area: State and/or MSA	High-Tech Workers (Sample N)	High-Tech Workers (percent)	Prominent High-Tech Industries
West	San Jose, California	1871	17.5	Electrical machinery; Computers
	Brazoria, Texas	162	14.7	Petrochemicals
	Sante Fe-Los Alamos, New Mexico	82	11.1	Commercial R&D labs
Southeast	Johnson City and Kingsport, Tennessee; Bristol, Virginia	94	12.7	Plastics and synthetics; Radio-TV
	Knoxville, Tennessee (part)	211	10.8	Plastics and synthetics
	Huntsville, Alabama	177	10.6	Electrical machinery; Missiles, space vehicles
Midwest	Columbus, Indiana	110	17.8	Engines and turbines
	Wichita, Kansas	491	16.7	Aircraft and parts
	Kokomo, Indiana	142	13.1	Radio, TV, and communications equipment
Northeast	Rochester, New York	891	19.8	Photographic equipment
	Burlington, Vermont	152	13.8	Electrical machinery
	Manchester, Portsmouth-Dover-Rochester, New Hampshire	484	13.3	Electrical machinery

Industrial Diversification

Though certain high-tech industries are common to all regions (Table 4.2.), a regional division of labor in terms of industries is apparent in these data on high-tech centers. All regions have concentrations of high-tech workers in the radio, TV, and communications equipment and electrical machinery industry groups. Beyond these industries, however, regional specialization of high-tech centers is evident. Plastics and synthetics, industrial chemicals, guided missiles and space vehicles, and computer and data processing services industries are concentrated in the Southeastern centers. Electronic computing equipment, guided missiles and space vehicles, scientific and controlling instruments, commercial research and development test labs, and computer and data processing services industries characterize high-tech employment in the Western centers. The Midwest region has its highest unique concentrations of high-tech workers in engines, turbines, and aircraft manufacturing. Specific to the Northeast is a high proportion of high-tech workers in photographic equipment and supplies industries.

Occupational Distributions

Table 4.3 compares the occupational distributions of high-tech and other workers in the twelve high-tech labor market areas. In contrast to other industries, high-tech industries exhibit higher concentrations of engineers, scientists, technicians, and production workers (see the analysis in chapter 3). The data suggest that a two-tiered occupational structure with proportionally fewer middle-range workers (sales, clerical, and administrative support) characterizes high-tech employment in these labor markets.

High-tech occupational distributions are displayed by region in Table 4.4, and the data allow us to assess the spatial separation of technical and production workers. While the best evaluation of this notion would require firm-level data, occupational specialization within regions can be indicative of this separation and is apparent even in aggregated data (note particularly the West and Midwest regions).

High-tech centers in the West exceed all other regions in concentrations of high-tech workers in managerial and administrative positions (17 percent as compared to 5 percent in the Midwest region). Professionals (engineers, scientists, and others) are also highly concentrated among the high-tech workers in Western labor markets and

Table 4.2   Industrial Distribution of High-Tech Workers
by U.S. Region (in percentages)

Industry	Southeast	West	Midwest	Northeast
Plastics, synthetics, and resins	26.8	1.0	0.7	1.0
Drugs	2.3	.9	.3	1.5
Industrial and misc. chemicals	11.6	6.4	2.2	1.6
Ordnance	3.3	1.0	1.9	2.6
Engine and turbines	0.6	0.2	14.0	0.3
Office and accounting machines	0.8	0.7	0.3	0.9
Electronic computing equipment	3.5	19.1	1.2	7.3
Radio, TV, and communications equipment	22.0	7.4	11.4	8.4
Electrical machinery, equipment, and supplies, n.e.c.	12.2	30.6	7.9	18.5
Aircraft and parts	0.2	1.1	54.5	3.0
Guided missiles, space vehicles, and parts	6.2	8.6	0.7	0.3
Scientific and controlling instruments	0.2	6.0	1.2	5.0
Optical and health services supplies	1.2	2.1	0.3	5.9
Photographic equipment and supplies	0.6	0.7	0.0	40.5
Commercial research and development, test labs	1.0	6.0	0.1	0.7
Business management and consulting services	1.2	3.4	1.6	1.0
Computer and data processing services	6.0	5.0	1.7	1.4

least concentrated in the Midwest high-tech centers. Moreover, the Midwest's high-tech workers are clustered in production jobs (skilled, semiskilled, and laborer). The smallest percentage of workers in these jobs is evident in the West. A clear spatial separation between higher-tier professional and technical personnel and lower-tier production personnel exists between high-tech centers in the West and those in the Midwest regions.

Table 4.3   Occupational Distribution of High-Tech and Other Workers (in percentages)

Occupation	High-Tech Workers	Other Workers
Executive, administrative, and managerial	12.0	12.1
Professionals: Engineers and scientists	13.9	2.1
Professionals: Other professional specialities	2.5	10.8
Technicians and related support personnel	10.0	2.8
Sales and administrative support including clerical	16.8	25.5
Service	1.8	10.0
Farming, forestry, and fishing	0.0	3.3
Precision production, craft and repair	18.2	15.8
Machine operators, assemblers, transporters, handlers, laborers	25.7	17.6
*Total percent	100	100
Total N	4867	21088

*Total percent does not equal 100 due to rounding error.

The Southeast and the Northeast display similar occupational distributions falling midway between the extreme percentages shown for the West and Midwest regions. Consistent with our expectations, the high-tech labor force in the Southeast is more concentrated in lower skill production jobs.

Table 4.4 Occupational Distribution of High-Tech Workers in High-Tech Centers by U. S. Region (in percentages)

Occupational Group	Southeast	West	Midwest	Northeast
Executive, administrative, and managerial	9.1	17.1	5.7	9.1
Professionals: Engineers and scientists	9.5	18.2	7.1	12.6
Professionals: Other profesional specialties	1.7	3.2	1.9	2.1
Technicians and related support	8.1	11.7	4.4	8.1
Sales and administrative support, including clerical	12.9	18.4	14.8	16.9
Service	2.5	1.8	1.2	1.8
Farming, forestry, and fishing	0.0	0.0	0.0	0.1
Precision production, craft, and repair	14.5	16.0	25.7	18.7
Machine operators, assemblers, transporters, handlers, and laborers	41.7	13.7	39.2	30.6
Total N	482	2115	743	1527

Summary of Our Findings

These data from the 1980 Census provide some support for Castells's notion about the location of high-tech industries and the spatial division of labor. Military and space facilities as well as research universities are linked to the location of certain high-tech centers. An absence of a tradition of unionization tends to attract high-tech industries. Though these data do not directly speak to the availability of venture capital, documented patterns of high-risk financing correspond in a timely way to growth in high-tech industries in underdeveloped areas. Finally, the separation of technical and professional personnel from production workers in high-tech industries is most prominent between the West and Midwest regions. These seemingly pivotal factors in location are distinctive to the high-tech industrial sector which appears to depart from other industrial sectors in terms of location, industrial, and occupational patterns.

Comparison with Other Research

These findings in large measure support certain conclusions reached by other researchers concerning spatial patterns of high-tech industries. First, our findings conform to Glasmeier's study in which she notes that geographic pattern of occupational dispersion among high-tech workers across states.[48] Similarly, Markusen and Bloch's study of defense-related high-tech firms reports the spatial separation of high-skilled and low-skilled workers as well as of professional, technical, and scientific workers.[49] Second, particular high-tech industries tend to concentrate in particular regions. In our research, regional concentrations of employment include plastics in the Southeast; electronic computing equipment and data processing services in the West; aircraft in the Midwest region; and photographic equipment in the Northeast. Glasmeier and co-workers also document highly concentrated employment patterns for certain high-tech industries, particularly those relating to the space and defense industries. Third, still other high-tech industries are more geographically dispersed than others. In our research employment in electrical machinery, equipment and supplies, and to a lesser extent radio, TV, and communications equipment are distributed throughout all four regions. This finding is corroborated by Glasmeier and co-workers' study of various high-tech industries and Robert Sklar's study of the electronics industry.[50] The latter reports that by 1983, thirty-four states had one or more electronics plants, and Colorado, Illinois, Massachusetts, New Jersey, New York, Pennsylvania and Texas had over 1000 such facilities.

A final pattern that cannot be ascertained in our analysis but is documented by Sklar, Glasmeier and co-workers, and Falk and Lyson concerns the rural or urban location of high-tech firms.[51] Sklar notes that many electronics plants are not located in high-tech centers but in small communities and rural areas around the country. Despite this finding, it is apparent from our research as well as that of others that high-tech industries are still generally found in urban areas. Glasmeier and co-workers report that over 80 percent of all high-tech employment is located in 264 SMSAs. These researchers also found that small to medium SMSAs displayed the sharpest percent changes in high-tech employment and are consequently more dependent on high-tech firms. This is a finding partially corroborated in our analysis.

The Falk and Lyson study of industrial patterns in the South addresses the rural and urban differences in high-tech location by comparing employment patterns among four types of county groups: SMSAs, other urban, rural white, and black belt. They find that slightly over 10 percent of Southern high-tech employment is located in rural areas and that, of the new high-tech jobs added to this region's economy from 1977 to 1981, less than 6 percent were located in rural areas. They conclude that the gap between rural and urban areas in high-tech employment has actually increased in recent years.[52]

CONCLUSIONS

At the outset of this chapter, we noted the important economic and national security implications that many attribute to the high-tech sector. These technologically oriented industries are considered crucial for the renaissance of U.S. industrial competitiveness. It is not surprising, then, that there has been much attention and energy focused on high-tech industrial development. Our analysis of this development has centered on its implications for the spatial division of labor. Using a restructuring approach that contains both neoclassical and radical elements, we have identified and explained certain patterns of high-tech development.

In our analysis as well as that of others, it is apparent that high-tech industries have not joined many established industries in the United States in rushing to the Sunbelt. While high-tech centers in the Southeast were identified in this research, the high-tech share of the local labor force was lower in Southeastern high-tech centers than elsewhere. The restructuring perspective seems to provide the most plausible explanation for the distinctive spatial configuration generated by this new expanding industrial sector.

The restructuring approach emphasizes natural *and* social constraints that produce a spatial division of labor. The perspective also focuses on the reciprocal relationship between industries and the labor markets in which they locate. Clearly, high-tech industries have responded favorably to sites that offer research capabilities and the availability of technically trained personnel. Moreover, high-tech industries have also cultivated area characteristics conducive to their success in given locales. Huntsville, Alabama provides one example of the reciprocal process of area development. Redstone Arsenal and NASA's Marshall Space Flight Center were surely the impetus for high-tech development in this area. A wide range of defense and space-related firms located in Huntsville to exploit increased postwar federal spending in these industries. Yet, the availability of technically trained personnel in the region was limited, and community pressure was exerted to create a regional university with strong technical programs to support this growing high-tech sector. The University of Alabama in Huntsville is a product of this pressure, and it strongly emphasizes engineering and other technical fields.

Our research also corroborates earlier findings of uneven development within the high-tech industrial sector. There exists a spatial division of labor along particular (industry) and detailed (occupational) dimensions. Regions may share concentrations of industries such as electronics and radio, T.V. and communications, but regional specialization occurs in other high-tech industries.

Detailed or occupational divisions of labor are also important for understanding the spatial division of labor in high-tech industries. Clear divisions between technical and professional workers and production and assembly workers are evident across regions, between rural and urban areas, and within high-tech centers. This separation should not be understood solely on the basis of product cycle stages. Spatial separation is a product of different relations of production manifested in the bargaining power of workers and employers that accompany various stages of product cycles. While technological considerations make the separation possible, social relations of production serve as a basis for dividing workers. In the early stages of product development, the necessity of close communication and exchange between technical and administrative personnel will produce clustering of these activities in certain high-tech centers, especially in the Northeast and West. The static flexibility approach to production of many high-tech products has resulted in the creation of a low-skill, low-wage labor force with little bargaining power whose numbers and location can easily be altered. High-tech centers in the Southeast and Midwest regions provide such conditions. The cyclical pattern of uneven development is apparent in the emergence of high-tech industrialization in declining areas like the Northeast or Midwest regions.

The high-tech industrial sector provides employment for less than 10 percent of American workers. It is a growing sector, however, and highly sought after by many areas in the competition for economic development. Despite concerted efforts and carefully planned strategies, research suggests that some locations are not necessarily attractive to high-tech industry. Even those areas attractive to other industries may not be enticing to high-tech industries.

High-tech industries have the greatest impact through applications of innovations that lead to growth in consumer demand and new employment in other industrial sectors. The movement of high-tech firms into an area can also alter the local infrastructure, spurring investment in education, services, and public works. Nonetheless, it is important to acknowledge the uncertainties and vulnerabilities in high-tech products, markets, employment, and firms. High-tech firms must rest upon an established stable economic base. The human capital requirements of high-tech firms—a highly trained labor force along with an economic, political, and social atmosphere conducive to innovation—are often built on existing local strengths, such as a university, defense base, or space center. Finally, we reiterate that the number of jobs directly and indirectly created by high-tech industries has not and is not likely soon to accommodate vast numbers of U.S. workers. The great potential for economic progress and expansion that high-tech industrialization promises must be tempered by its limited track record for providing employment, job security, and economic advantages to a few specific locales.

Chapter Five

Earnings and Inequality in High-Tech Industries: National, Regional, and Local Patterns

In the last two chapters we have examined the technical, social, and spatial divisions of labor in high-tech industries. We have found it useful to employ a restructuring perspective and to identify signs of static and dynamic flexibility. We now turn to socioeconomic consequences of these divisions of labor in high-tech industries—particularly those of earnings and earnings inequality. These consequences are important for understanding local, regional, and national trends in the distribution of economic advantages and disadvantages. There is substantial evidence of increasing inequality and polarization of income in American society in recent years.[1] We show that, while the level of earnings inequality within high-tech industries is no greater than other sectors, there are interesting if not disturbing patterns in the technology sector that may be precursors of trends elsewhere in the U.S. industrial structure.

Certain features of high-tech industries are of particular importance for the sectoral wage determination process. Strategies of static and dynamic flexibility employed in high-tech industries influence the earnings distribution of high-tech workers. At the firm level, the distribution of wages is integrally linked to the bargaining power of workers, and the after-cost profits that are available to distribute as wages.[2] Strategies of static flexibility that prevail in U.S. high-tech firms affect the bargaining power of workers at different levels of the occupational hierarchy through the elasticities of demand for labor. Static strategies include outsourcing or the mobility of production, deskilling, eliminating jobs through automation, using minority workers to fill less-skilled positions, using ancillary workers to lower labor costs, and using contingency management practices. All of these measures influence elasticities in the demand for labor. On the one hand, elasticities are very high for lower-tier production workers who are often minorities. On the other hand, demand for labor in the upper tier of professional, technical, and managerial workers—mostly white males—is very inelastic. When the demand for labor is more elastic or flexible, workers have less bargaining power and lower wages. In high-tech industries where elasticities vary by occupation, race, gender, and region, we can expect polarized patterns of earnings inequality corresponding to these divisions of labor.

Lack of unionization, labor intensiveness of production, and high price elasticities of many high-tech products also contribute to relatively lower wages for lower-tier workers compared to upper-tier workers. This pattern is most apparent among the more competitive industries within the high-tech sector such as radio and television. High profit levels achieved by successful high-tech firms raise the aggregate wage levels of high-tech workers, however, making high-tech industries attractive to highly skilled professionals and relatively unskilled workers alike.

Thus, though earnings in high-tech industries should be above average, we expect to find relatively polarized earnings distributions among high-tech workers due to a two-tier occupational structure. These general patterns may be mitigated by contextual effects such as region and local labor market type. Also, different types of industries within the high-tech sector vary in their use of flexible production strategies. While static flexibility characterizes most high-tech industries, some exhibit elements of a more dynamic approach to the flexibility issue. High-tech industries also differ in terms of market structures (competitive versus oligopolistic), elasticities of product demand, and degree of unionization. All of these factors can effect the socioeconomic returns to workers within the high-tech sector.

Our initial analyses of earnings and inequality compare high-tech workers with other workers on a national basis. Industry and occupation (which define the technical division of labor) and gender, race, and ethnicity (which constitute the social division of labor) are of primary concern in this analysis. Using Current Population Survey data on U.S. labor forces from 1970 to 1987, we compare average earnings and earnings inequality of high-tech workers with their peers in other industries.[3] Then differences within the high-tech sector between industries, occupations, and social segments of the labor force are noted.

EARNINGS AND INEQUALITY IN THE HIGH-TECH LABOR FORCE:
A NATIONAL PROFILE

Earnings in High-Tech and Other Sectors

One of the reasons that high-tech industries are attractive to industrial recruiters and workers alike is higher average earnings levels. As illustrated in the third chapter, high-tech industries tend to employ more management, professional, and technical workers than other industries. Thus, one reason for higher average earnings in these industries is the concentration of upper-tier workers. Since highly trained technical and professional workers can be mobile in external as well as internal labor markets, exceptional earnings, benefits, and working conditions are viewed as essential for recruitment and retention. Even production workers tend to get slightly higher pay than their peers in other industrial sectors. These differences in earnings levels between high-tech workers and other industry workers are clearly shown in Figure 5.1.

On a national scale, throughout the 1970s and 1980s, high-tech workers have done well economically. Their average earnings have remained considerably higher than those of workers in service, manufacturing, and other U.S. industries. Furthermore, the gap between high-tech and other sectors appears to be widening in recent years. We attribute this to dramatic proportional reductions in blue-collar jobs in the high-tech labor force and to proportional increases in professional, managerial, and technical personnel (see chapter 3). Outsourcing and automation are undoubtedly responsible for much of the decline in lower-tier high-tech employment. Competitive pressure for research and development and increasing bureaucratization in an expanding sector accounts for some of the growth of upper-tier jobs that leads to the earnings differentials in Figure 5.1.

Also of interest are cyclical variations in the economy, the effects of which are evident in the average earnings of all sectors over time. Interestingly, declines in earnings during the recessions of the early 1970s and early 1980s are more dramatic for high-tech workers. This demonstrates the very volatile market environment faced by most high-tech industries and the greater requirement for flexibility in this sector.

Earnings Inequality

Using a standard measure of inequality—variance in the natural log of earnings—we examine earnings inequality in Figure 5.2. When

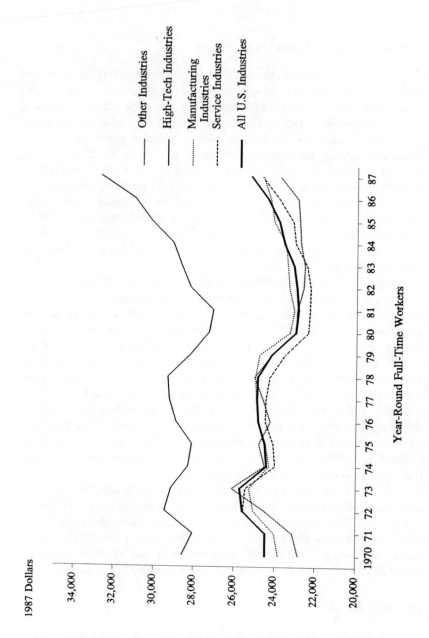

Figure 5.1   Earnings by Industry Sector from 1970 to 1987

compared to the heterogeneous category of all other industries, high-tech industries exhibit less overall earnings inequality. Every year from 1971 through 1986, the high-tech sector has less overall inequality. Like other sectors, that inequality appears to be increasing throughout the 1980s. The rate of increase in high-tech inequality, however, appears greater than other industries after 1980. We suspect that shifts in the high-tech sector's divisions of labor in recent years are contributing to the growth of inequality within these industries.

To evaluate this argument, we examine the roles of the social division of labor (race, gender, and ethnicity differences) and the technical division of labor (occupational differences) in generating earnings inequality for high-tech industries and for all other industries combined. Using a two-way analysis of variance for each year (1970 to 1987), we partition the variance of logged earnings into components due to a two-tiered pair of occupational categories (managers, professionals, and technical workers versus all others) and minority labor force status (blacks, Hispanics, and females versus white males). This partitioning allows us to decompose the earnings inequality into percent inequality due to occupation and percent inequality due to minority labor force status. These percentages are plotted for each year in Figure 5.3 and suggest some interesting, but disturbing, trends.

The variance in inequality due to minority status and occupational differences is considerably higher among high-tech industries than other industries. Sectoral trends are similar as the effect of minority status decreases for high-tech and other industries. Similarly, the effects of occupation on inequality decrease initially through the late 1970s, but then increase throughout the 1980s.

We believe the larger contributions of race and gender to inequality in high-tech industries may be traced to static flexibility strategies in which minority workers are restricted to lower paying jobs. This intersection of the high-tech technical and social divisions of labor is a prominent feature of the sector demonstrated in chapter 3. Compared to other industrial sectors, high-tech industries employ a much larger percent of minorities in blue-collar positions and a much smaller percent of minorities in professional, technical, and managerial positions. The consequences of this social division of labor are clear when we examine the bases of earnings inequality in which minority status accounts for between 8 and 16 percent of all inequality in the high-tech sector compared to 6 to 9 percent in all other industries over time.

Occupational differences, or the technical division of labor, are important for understanding earnings inequality. This is increasingly the case for the high-tech sector in the last decade. By 1983, variance

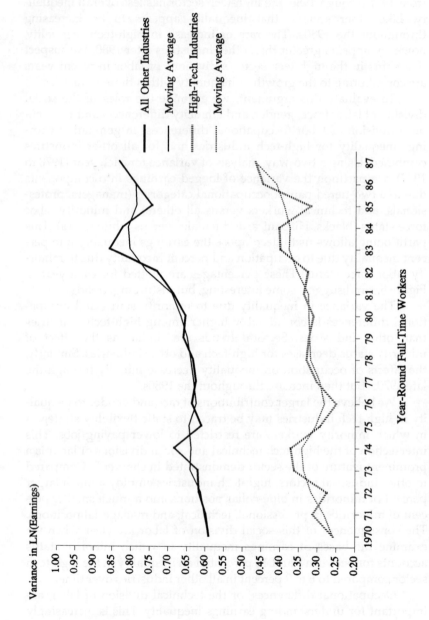

Figure 5.2 Earnings Inequality in High-Tech and All Other Industries

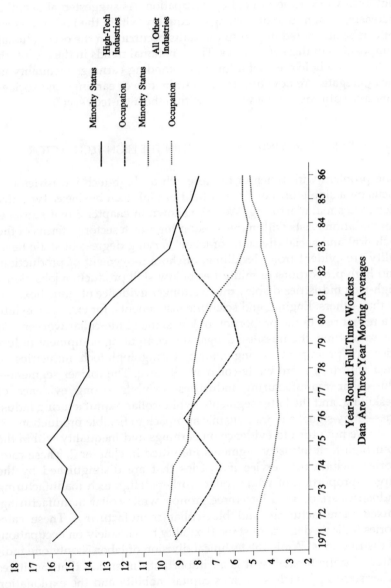

Percent

Minority Status — High-Tech Industries

Occupation — High-Tech Industries

Minority Status ⋯⋯ All Other Industries

Occupation ⋯⋯ All Other Industries

Figure 5.3 Earnings Inequality Due to Minority Status and Occupation

Year-Round Full-Time Workers
Data Are Three-Year Moving Averages

in earnings inequality due to the occupational structure outweighs that for minority status, with over 9 percent of total inequality among high-tech workers accounted by occupation. As suggested above, the increasing magnitude of earnings inequality within the high-tech sector can be attributed in part to the shifts occurring in the occupational composition of these industries. These national trends in the high-tech sector as a whole are useful for understanding earnings inequality in the aggregate. We now turn to an examination of earnings and socioeconomic patterns among workers within the high-tech sector.

EARNINGS AND INEQUALITY WITHIN THE HIGH-TECH SECTOR

One problem with much of the research on high-tech industries is a focus on a single firm or limited field of high-tech business, typically electronics manufacturing. We have shown in chapter 3 that substantial variation exists within the broader high-tech sector in terms of the technical and social divisions of labor. Varying degrees of static flexibility are evident from deskilling, offshore movement of production, and high proportions of minorities in low-skill production jobs. Some high-tech industries display much stronger evidence of static flexibility than others. Engines and scientific instruments, for example, exhibit a recent rise in the proportion of less-skilled blue-collar workers. At the same time, the missiles, drugs, and computing equipment industries are prominent among manufacturing high-tech industries in their shift to a more white-collar work force. The former segment—blue-collar manufacturing industries—exhibits strong evidence of deskilling, and the latter segment—white-collar manufacturing industries—may signal a more dynamic approach to flexible production.

We now turn to evidence on earnings and inequality within the four high-tech industry segments identified in chapter 3. These categories include the service industries that are distinguished by the largest proportion of white-collar workers. High-tech manufacturing industries are divided into three groups: white-collar manufacturing, mixed manufacturing, and blue-collar manufacturing. These categories indicate degrees of static flexibility based solely on occupational distributions. While the technical division of labor is only one indicator of static flexibility, it is an important dimension that facilitates other static approaches, such as capital mobility and the exploitation of minorities and temporary workers. We expect that the more an industry is characterized by static flexibility, the lower that industry's average earnings, the greater the earnings inequality, and the greater the roles of occupation, race, and gender in generating earnings inequality among workers. And to some extent, our expectations are realized in the following analyses.

Earnings in the High-Tech Sector

The average earnings of workers in each of the four high-tech segments is displayed in Figure 5.4. As expected, workers in the two segments with proportionally more white-collar positions have mean earnings several thousand dollars higher than workers in high-tech industries where blue-collar jobs dominate. Trends for workers in all four industry categories fluctuate with cyclical changes in the overall economy but generally rise throughout the 1980s after declining in the 1970s. These data add support to our notion that higher average earnings in the high-tech sector are in large part due to the high proportion of white-collar workers. The trend for blue-collar manufacturing high-tech industries is very similar to the trend for non–high-tech manufacturing industries as shown in Figure 5.1.

Earnings Inequality

Despite our use of moving averages, patterns of inequality within the high-technology sector are quite volatile over time, as indicated in Figure 5.5 Most of the volatility is due to sampling error associated with small sample sizes for some segments in some years. Inequalities among all three manufacturing segments are distinctly lower than that for high-tech service industries. However, for industry segments with more white-collar employees (service and manufacturing), the trend is toward constant or lower inequality through the 1980s. For industry segments with more blue-collar workers—those industries we consider most likely to be statically flexible—inequalities clearly rise during the 1980s. In fact, the blue-collar manufacturing segment has the lowest level of initial inequality and displays the sharpest increase in the last years plotted, eventually exceeding that of white-collar manufacturing.

To understand the basis for these inequalities in high-tech divisions of labor, we consider the effects of race, gender, and ethnicity in shaping total earnings inequality in each of the four high-tech segments. Moving averages of the percent of inequality accounted for by minority status are plotted in Figure 5.6. While the trends in earnings variance due to minority labor force status tend to a decline across time, there are some important differences among high-tech industry

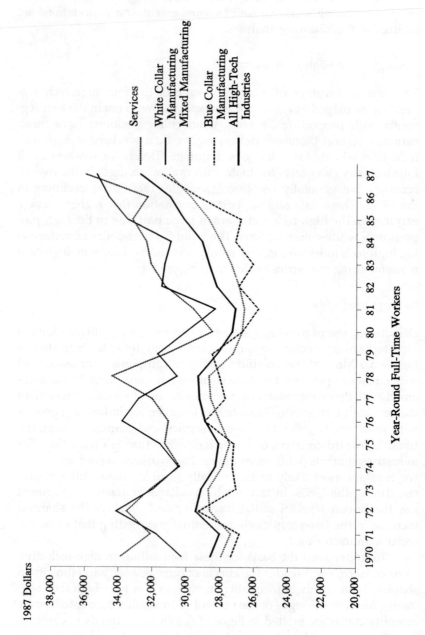

Figure 5.4 Earnings in High-Tech Industry Segments

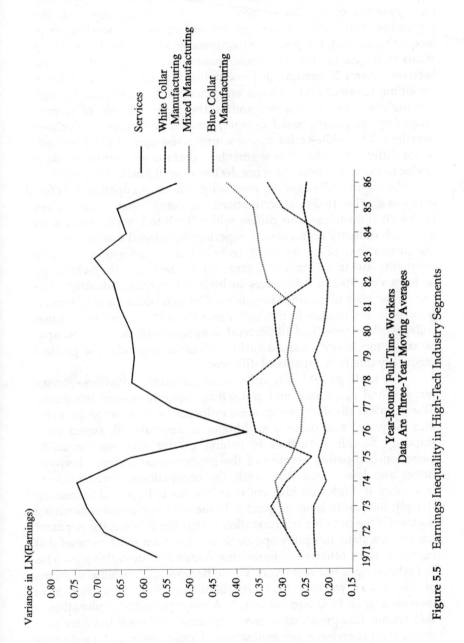

Figure 5.5 Earnings Inequality in High-Tech Industry Segments

segments. In line with our original hypothesis, the data suggest that the larger the blue-collar component in an industry segment, the higher the contribution of race, gender, and ethnicity to total earnings inequality. Indeed, the percent of variance accounted for by minority status is largest for the blue-collar manufacturing segment, ranging between 15 and 20 percent for those industries that strongly evidence deskilling (engines and turbines and scientific instruments). Though the high-tech service sector exhibits the highest levels of overall inequality, inequality based on race, gender, and ethnicity declines overtime. The white-collar manufacturing segment of the high-tech sector differs from the other segments in that the amount of inequality due to minority status does not decline overall during the period.

As Figure 5.7 suggests, inequality due to occupational differences—i.e., the two-tier occupational structure that characterizes high-tech industries—also differs within high-tech segments. As all high-tech industry segments are experiencing a trend toward increasing proportions of professional, technical, and managerial workers, inequality due to occupation is generally on the rise in the technology sector. Occupational differences in high-tech service industries contribute the least to earnings inequality. This is no doubt due to limited occupational variation in this sector and the relative absence of blue-collar workers (less than 10 percent). It appears that the most occupationally "top-heavy" manufacturing industries engender the greatest inequality due to occupational differences.

The findings for white-collar manufacturing industries—drugs, missiles and spacecraft, and computing equipment—are intriguing. This segment displays the greatest influence of occupation on earnings inequality and poses something of an anomaly. We expect more statically flexible industries to exhibit greater earnings inequality based on occupation because of the greater social distance between upper and lower tiers. But, while the occupational contribution to inequality in high-tech blue-collar industries is high and increasing sharply, inequality is not as great as in the white-collar manufacturing segment. One possible interpretation is that the white-collar segment has taken a static flexibility approach and has been most successful at outsourcing or otherwise eliminating domestic blue-collar jobs. This hypothesis does not seem very viable because the absolute numbers of blue-collar workers in white-collar high-tech industries have increased since 1970 (see Table 3.2). A more plausible explanation is that within this presumably more dynamic high-tech industry segment, the progressive reorganization of production and productive relations has yet to alter the wage structure.

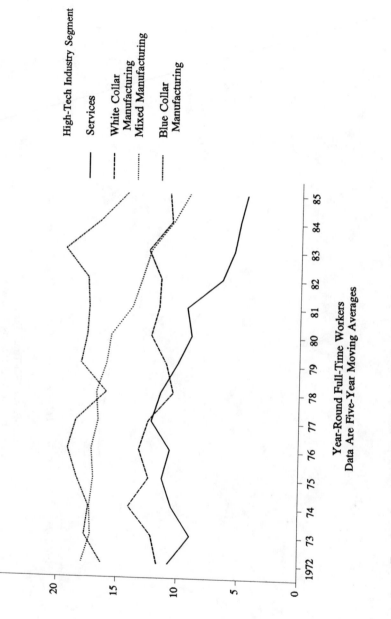

Figure 5.6 Earnings Inequality Due to Minority Labor Force Status

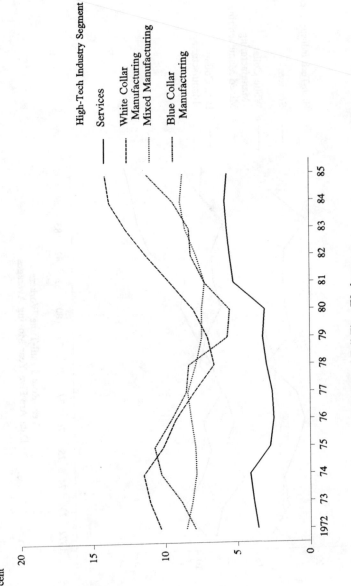

Figure 5.7 Earnings Inequality Due to Occupation

We conclude from these analyses that, with one notable exception, high-tech industries exhibit a variety of socioeconomic patterns that reflect a static approach to flexible production. The strongest evidence of static flexibility is found in average earnings levels and inequality due to race, gender, and ethnicity. Earnings levels are considerably lower for high-tech industries with large blue-collar components, and minority labor force status is more important in explaining earnings inequality in these industry segments than in others. Nonetheless, we consider our efforts exploratory. Other contingencies that affect wages and earnings inequality among workers in high-tech industries must be identified if we are to understand more fully the basis for the patterns we and others have observed.

These analyses underscore the importance of technical and social divisions of labor in generating earnings levels and inequality. A third, spatial division of labor is also critical for understanding patterns of employment, earnings, and inequality within the high-tech sector. We now turn to this spatial division of labor, examining its effects on socioeconomic outcomes of high-tech workers in different regions and in different local labor market contexts.

SPATIAL EFFECTS ON EARNINGS AND INEQUALITY OF HIGH-TECH WORKERS

The restructuring of the U.S. economy is not uniform, but a process of uneven development. One of the major consequences of the uneven development process is the exacerbation of economic inequality as certain regions, labor markets, industrial sectors, and groups of people accumulate advantages and disadvantages over time.[4] Considerable research has been done on the relationship between the economic structures of regions, communities, and labor markets and the socioeconomic outcomes experienced by residents and workers. Area differences in structure and outcomes have been demonstrated in studies by Hanusheck; Harrison; Fossett and Galle; Beck and Colclough; and Horan and Tolbert, among others.[5] Income, earnings, inequality, and the value of schooling have been linked to indicators of industrial structure such as percent of employment in oligopolistic or core industries,[6] manufacturing employment,[7] average manufacturing wages,[8] city size,[9] and a host of other factors.[10] The consistent conclusion of this research is that the organization of production within regions and local areas has a substantial effect on residents' well-being. While its influence may vary across subgroups of the population, the local social organization of production is a factor that must be taken into account.

We are not suggesting that economic structure alone determines individual earnings or the distribution of earnings in a given area. Sociological and economic research on earnings determination has demonstrated that many factors are important in determining economic well-being. These include individual-level human capital characteristics such as skill, training, and job experience as well as structural features like industrial sectors.[11] Consistent with previous research, our contention here is that a local area's particular social and economic history—i.e., its industrial mix, social relations of production, and class struggle—shapes the context in which human capital characteristics are developed and evaluated and in which wages are determined for different groups of workers. In so doing, this context shapes the technical, spatial, and social divisions of labor.

Industrial structure and development have a major impact on spatial and technical divisions of labor. Restructuring theorists argue that these divisions of labor evolve as management strategies change and through struggles between workers and employers over wages, autonomy, and job security. These conflicts take place within a context shaped by market structures, product-specific factors, and organizational traditions that define labor processes and labor relations. The result is the tendency for the technical division of labor (based on occupations and industries) to exhibit distinctive spatial tendencies. High-tech industries have their own spatial distributions of labor due to the outcomes of struggles over managerial strategies such as static and dynamic flexibility and the external contingencies of space and defense markets, technically oriented universities, union-free environments, and other factors that influence location decisions.

Yet, as the restructuring perspective suggests, these divisions of labor are not static. Local divisions of labor change over time as the locale itself adapts to further development. There can be local or regional growth or decline as well as cyclical or market-inspired changes in the bargaining power of workers and employers. This bargaining power will be reflected in the distributions of workers' earnings within industrial sectors and between sectors. For example, the location of certain high-tech firms in an area can alter the local economy through spinoff firms, the attraction of satellite businesses, and the support for local education and training facilities. This in turn can change the demand and supply for certain types of labor and influence managerial strategies for control within the firm. It is within the context of these processes that the power of workers and employers is exercised and altered, divisions of labor are created and changed, and socioeconomic outcomes are continuously being determined.

These technical and spatial divisions of labor are crosscut by the social division of labor, producing segmentation of labor by race, gender, and ethnicity. Most importantly, minority labor force status affects the power that both workers and employers bring into the labor process. This results in differential access to production positions and locations. The race, gender, and ethnic groups that reside in a given area are shaped into social divisions of labor through the location decisions of firms and the differential uses of social groups in meeting various labor needs. As noted in chapter 2, certain sites may be chosen by employers to exploit available labor sources composed of certain social groups such as women, blacks, or Hispanics. Locations may be shunned because of the organizing potential of certain categories of workers. Avoidance of Black Belt areas in the Southeast, for example, has been attributed to white employers' fear of political and union activity among black workers in these areas.[12] The complex interactions of these three divisions of labor—technical, spatial, and social—are played out not only in the workplace but across local, regional, and even national economies.

In the remainder of this chapter, we examine the consequences of these divisions of labor for socioeconomic inequalities among high-tech workers in regional and local economies. Initially, our spatial context includes twelve high-tech centers identified in chapter 4. We then focus on labor market areas that represent other types of local economies and compare these to high-tech areas.

REGIONAL VARIATIONS IN EARNINGS AND INEQUALITY
IN HIGH-TECH CENTERS

Using the Public Use Microdata Sample-D (PUMS-D) 1980 Census data and the regional high-tech centers identified in chapter 4, we now examine earnings levels, distributions, and inequalities among high-tech workers and other workers. It is well known that wages vary substantially from one region of the United States to another. The data in Table 5.1 indicate regional variability in mean earnings of high-tech workers in high-tech centers as well. The lowest average earnings for high-tech workers is in the Southeast, and the highest average is in the West. A similar pattern holds for other workers. The data also suggest that high-tech workers in every region have higher average earnings than their non–high-tech counterparts. Though high-tech industries may raise average wages in an area, they do not appear to alter relative earnings differentials that already exist between different regions of the country.

Table 5.1   Mean Earnings for High-Tech and Other Workers
Residing in High-Tech Labor Market Areas by U.S. Region

Region	High-Tech Workers	Other Workers	T-test
Southeast	15,278	12,417	5.90*
West	20,371	16,829	12.11*
Midwest	17,004	14,042	7.77*
Northeast	18,876	13,609	17.47*

*$p < 0.01$

Profiles of high-tech workers' earnings from the twelve high-tech centers are shown by region in Figures 5.8 and 5.9. Though regional differences are noticeable, a two-tier earnings profile is apparent for all regions except the Midwest where production and assembly jobs are most common for high-tech workers. Production workers account for large peaks at lower earnings levels, and highly skilled technical and professional workers account for smaller peaks at the highest tier of earnings. With the exception of the earnings profile for Western high-tech workers, the two-tier structure is more pronounced among high-tech workers in service industries. The polarized earnings distribution of high-tech workers, particularly those in manufacturing industries, is undoubtedly associated with the relative absence of middle-range occupational opportunities in these industries. The two-tier structure of earnings among high-tech service workers, however, cannot be as easily traced to its occupational structure because it is overwhelmingly white-collar. As we will see below, the explanation of inequality may lie in the social division of labor for high-tech service industries in these high-tech centers.

Earnings Inequality

To assess the magnitude of inequality in the high-tech centers' earnings distributions, we rely again on variance in log earnings used in the previous analysis. These coefficients are calculated within regions for various segments of high-tech and non high-tech labor forces. The

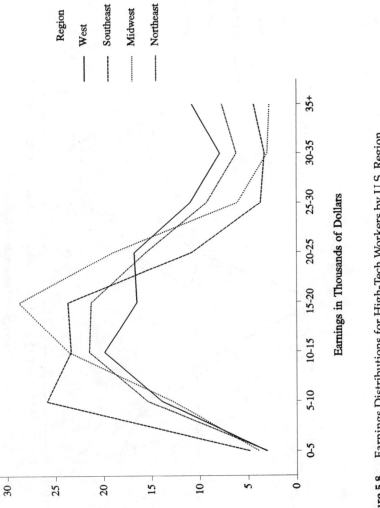

Percent of Workers

Region
West
Southeast
Midwest
Northeast

Earnings in Thousands of Dollars

Figure 5.8 Earnings Distributions for High-Tech Workers by U.S. Region

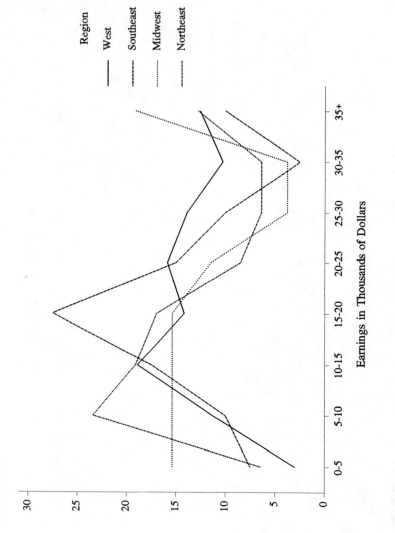

Figure 5.9   Earnings Distributions for High-Tech Service Workers by U.S. Region

lower the variance in Table 5.2, the less the extent of earnings inequality. Consistent with our findings for the national labor force, earnings inequality is greater among workers in sectors other than high-tech in each region. This is due to the very heterogeneous mix of occupations and industries represented by these workers. Inequality among high-tech workers is greatest in Western high-tech markets, followed by the Southeast, the Northeast and the Midwest. These earnings inequality patterns among high-tech workers both between and within regions correspond to the general patterns of inequality documented by other researchers. We suspect that the development of high-tech industries in the West and Southeast has produced greater disparities between upper- and lower-tier high-tech workers due to the lack of unions and lower average wages among workers in these regions.

Table 5.2   Earnings Inequality Among High-Tech and Other Industry Workers in High-Tech Market Areas in Four U.S. Regions

Region	Overall Inequality	Inequality Among High-Tech Workers	Inequality Among Other Workers
Southeast	0.540	0.416	0.550
No. of cases	3665	482	3183
West	0.571	0.426	0.594
No. of cases	10574	2114	8460
Midwest	0.570	0.360	0.604
No. of cases	3928	742	3186
Northeast	0.490	0.373	0.491
No. of cases	7652	1526	6126

When manufacturing workers from high-tech centers are compared to service workers in Table 5.3, we see that service industries tend to exhibit greater earnings inequality than do manufacturing industries. Inequality is most extreme among workers in high-tech, service industries—especially in the Midwest region.[13] Among regions, high-tech centers in the Southeast and particularly the West show less difference in inequalities among high-tech service workers and high-tech manufacturing workers. In contrast, the Northeast and Midwest regions exhibit greater earnings inequalities among high-tech service workers. One possible explanation for these patterns lies in the traditional strength of unions among manufacturing workers in these rustbelt regions. It follows that less unionized service industries would result in greater earnings inequality. Without a union legacy, the Sunbelt's manufacturing and service distinction has less influence on earnings inequality in these regions.

Table 5.3 Inequality Among Manufacturing and Service Workers for High-Tech and Other Industries By U.S. Region

Industry	Southeast	West	Midwest	Northeast
High-Tech				
Manufacturing	0.408	0.426	0.341	0.366
No. of cases	442	1813	717	1479
Service	0.473	0.420	0.974	0.602
No. of cases	40	301	25	47
Other Industries				
Manufacturing	0.590	0.511	0.339	0.407
No. of cases	952	1209	729	1407
Service	0.510	0.610	0.648	0.513
No. of cases	1846	6201	2051	4071
Other	0.637	0.579	0.773	0.507
No. of cases	385	1050	406	648

Racial and Gender Inequalities in Earnings

Using a one-way analysis of variance, earnings inequality can be decomposed into within-group and between-group components. This allows us to assess the effect of race and gender differences in earnings in the overall earnings inequality of workers residing in high-tech centers as shown in Table 5.4. The most obvious finding is that race and gender differences play a substantially larger role in shaping earnings inequality among high-tech workers than among other workers. The regional patterns displayed here are very consistent with the trend we observed above for the national high-tech sector. Unlike the previous analysis, race and gender differences are particularly notable among workers in high-tech service industries where the total inequality tends to be greater as well. One must keep in mind that this analysis concentrates solely on high-tech centers where these industries are most dominant, whereas the previous national analysis examined all high-tech workers. In the Midwest region, race and gender differences account for over 45 percent of the total earnings inequality among workers in high-tech service industries compared to only 19 percent among other service industry workers. Small sample sizes make coefficients for high-tech service workers less reliable in all regions except the West.

Table 5.4 Percent of Total Inequality Due to Race and Gender for High-Tech and Other Industries by U.S. Region

Industry	Southeast	West	Midwest	Northeast
High-Tech				
Manufacturing	14.1	22.3	11.1	22.8
Service	31.7	26.3	45.4	31.9
Other Industries				
Manufacturing	9.6	13.9	15.8	15.2
Service	12.4	11.1	19.3	12.6
Other	5.2	10.7	3.0	5.2

We suspect that the findings relating to high-tech manufacturing industries can be attributed in part to the technical division of labor in this sector. We have demonstrated that high-tech industries have particularly large concentrations of engineers, scientists, and technicians; very few clerical and sales positions; and large numbers of production and assembly personnel. However, the social division of labor is important as well. The top levels of these uncommon occupational structures consist primarily of male-dominated occupations. Middle-range clerical jobs that traditionally exhibit higher concentrations of female workers are few in number. In the typical approach of static flexibility, minority workers with limited bargaining power and few alternative employment opportunities are found in production jobs. In addition to our own analyses in chapter 3, the research of Falk and Lyson on high-tech industries in the South corroborates these assumptions. They report that white males are vastly overrepresented in professional, technical, and managerial occupations while minorities are more concentrated in craft and operative jobs.[14]

Summary

The patterns of earnings and inequality among high-tech workers in high-tech centers vary by region and differ from those of other workers in the centers we sampled. Again, on the average, high-tech workers receive higher pay than other workers. Regional variation in high-tech earnings is similar to that of other industries. For the most part, a polarized earnings profile exists among high-tech workers that is exacerbated when these workers are employed in high-tech service industries. Race and gender contributions to total earnings inequality among high-tech workers are substantial and exceed the corresponding contributions to total inequality for non–high-tech workers in all regions.

This analysis has been confined to high-tech centers in four regions of the United States. Because high technology plays a more integral role in these labor market areas, our focus on high-tech centers reveals distinctive area characteristics. But, of course, high-tech industries also locate outside these technology centers. We now turn to a consideration of high-tech industries outside high-tech centers where the sector is not a dominant feature of the local labor market.

EARNINGS AND INEQUALITY ACROSS DIFFERENT TYPES OF LABOR MARKETS

This analysis examines earnings and inequalities among Southeastern high-tech and other workers in a variety of labor market types.[15] To reduce the confounding effects of region, we focus solely on the Southeast in this analysis. This is a particularly interesting region because of its diversified set of high-tech industries and the rapid growth of this sector in recent years. Employing the PUMS-D Census data, we have selected twelve labor markets, three markets for each of four types. The Southeastern labor markets are characterized by the highest levels of employment in manufacturing, services, agriculture, and high technology in the region. The high-tech market areas are the same three we have used above.

Figure 5.10 displays the market areas chosen to represent the four different types of local economies. The high-tech market areas consist of the Morristown-Greenville, Huntsville, and Johnson City–Bristol City–Kingsport areas. It is important to note that even in these technology centers, the percent of employment in high tech is no more than 13 percent. This small percentage sharply contrasts to the near 50 percent of manufacturing employment in labor markets that we label manufacturing economies. Known for their furniture and textile industries, the Hickory, North Carolina, and Columbus and Dalton, Georgia, market areas epitomize manufacturing in the Southeast. All of the service market areas are in Florida: Gainesville, Jacksonville, and Tallahassee. In each case, service employment encompasses an overwhelming majority of the labor force (more than 75 percent). Of the three agricultural areas, one is found in southern Kentucky. The other markets with the most agricultural employment are in the Mississippi delta area, one on the Arkansas side of the river and the other on the Mississippi side.

Earnings Inequality

Our previous findings that high-tech workers enjoy significantly higher average earnings than other workers hold across other labor market types with the exception of agriculturally based local economies, as shown in Table 5.5. Here average earnings between high-tech workers and others are much the same. In our earlier analysis, we found that earnings inequality is lower among high-tech workers than other workers in high-tech centers. This is not the case in labor markets dominated by manufacturing. When we compare the variances, inequality actually appears higher for high-tech workers in manufacturing-dominated labor markets, as shown in Table 5.6. In all other labor market types, inequality is greater among non–high-tech workers.

Table 5.5   Mean Earnings for Southeastern Labor Market Area Types: High-Tech Versus Other Workers

Market Area Type	High-Tech Workers	Other Workers	T-test
High-Tech	15,278	12,417	5.90*
Manufacturing	14,660	11,500	2.96*
Service	15,773	13,209	2.12**
Agricultural	10,492	10,695	-0.16

*p < 0.01
**p < 0.05

We can attribute some of the differences in earnings inequality among high-tech workers in different labor market types to variance in industrial and occupational composition of high-tech industries in each of these labor market types. As noted above, the industrial mix

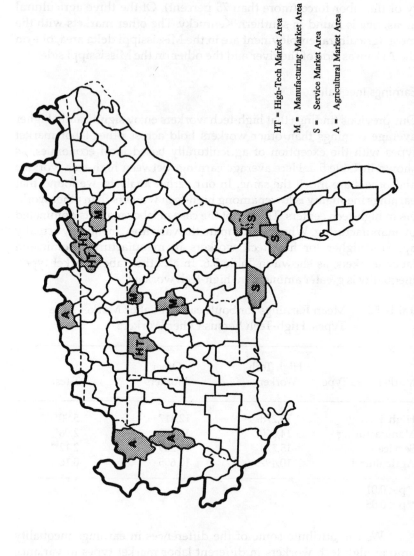

Figure 5.10   High-Tech, Manufacturing, Service, and Agricultural Labor Market Areas in the South: 1980

HT = High-Tech Market Area

M = Manufacturing Market Area

S = Service Market Area

A = Agricultural Market Area

of high-tech industries in high-tech centers is more diverse, including both service and manufacturing sectors. In labor markets dominated by general service industries, we find the highest proportions of high-tech, service employment (29 percent). Manufacturing-based labor markets in the Southeast tend to employ the largest percentage of high-tech workers in electrical machinery industries (57 percent), where standardized production jobs provide the bulk of high-tech employment opportunities. Finally, in the Southeastern agriculture market areas, high-tech service industries are few, and manufacturing dominates high-tech employment. The key industries are drugs (employing 33 percent), communications equipment (33 percent), and to a lesser extent electrical machinery (19 percent).

Table 5.6 Earnings Inequality in Four Types of Southeastern Labor Market Areas

Market Type	Overall Inequality	Inequality Among High-Tech Workers	Inequality Among Other Workers
High-Tech	0.540	0.416	0.550
No. of cases	3665	482	3183
Manufacturing	0.472	0.598	0.467
No. of cases	2730	74	2656
Service	0.527	0.386	0.529
No. of cases	3908	76	3832
Agricultural	0.646	0.221	0.665
No. of cases	1223	54	1169

The industrial composition of these labor markets influences the local technical divisions of high-tech labor. The common two-tier structure of managerial and professional jobs and production jobs in the high-tech labor force does not hold for all market types. Agricultural labor markets, distinguished above by their limited earnings inequality among high-tech workers, are also distinguished by their limited variation in high-tech jobs. Close to 80 percent of all high-tech workers occupy production positions while only 9 percent are managers or professionals. The greatest earnings inequality is among workers in manufacturing-dominated labor markets that exhibit a three-tiered occupational structure, spanning professional and technical positions, midlevel sales and clerical jobs, and a substantial production segment.

Industry and occupation explain some of the variations in earnings and inequality among high-tech workers in different types of labor markets, but not all differences. The unique history, location, and social and political context in which labor markets develop clearly shape the social and economic contours of high-tech employment.

Race and Gender Differences

Our previous analyses, and that of others, has noted extreme disparities between the employment situations of women, blacks, and certain ethnic groups and that of white males in high-tech industries. We reported above that substantial inequality in earnings is attributable to minority labor force status nationally and in high-tech centers in every U.S. region. The most pronounced inequality is in high-tech service industries in general and in the Midwest region in particular. Using a one-way analysis of variance, we assess the contribution of race and gender to earnings inequality in each of the four labor market types in Table 5.7. Once again, regardless of labor market type, race and gender differences contribute substantially more to earnings inequality among high-tech workers than among other workers. Contributions of race and gender groups to total earnings inequality among high-tech workers range from 15 to 25 percent, while among non–high-tech workers the range is 9 to 14 percent.

Table 5.7   Earnings Inequality Due to Race and Gender in Four
            Types of Southeastern Labor Market Areas

Market Type	Percent Inequality Due to Race and Gender
High-Tech	
High-Tech Workers	15.4
Other Workers	9.2
Manufacturing	
High-Tech Workers	24.7
Other Workers	11.8
Service	
High-Tech Workers	23.7
Other Workers	13.7

Table 5.7 *(continued)*

Market Type	Percent Inequality Due to Race and Gender
Agricultural	
High-Tech Workers	20.4
Other Workers	12.2

The economic inequality between minority groups and the majority in high-tech industries is the most consistent finding across all of our analyses. On national and regional levels, across service and manufacturing high-tech industries, and even in high-tech industries located outside technology centers, the economic disparities between different race and gender groups are extreme. They characterize a form of labor force segmentation that will become increasingly significant as high tech becomes a more dominant sector in the U.S. economy.

CONCLUSIONS

We have shown that various divisions of labor have distinct configurations in high-tech industries and that these divisions are clearly related to earnings and earnings inequality in this sector. Our analyses reveal above-average earnings for high-tech industries in the aggregate. This is a function of the top-heavy, two-tier occupation structure that consists of larger proportions of professional, technical, and managerial workers than other industrial sectors. Earnings inequality can be understood in part by flexible production regimes that manifest themselves in the high-tech sector primarily in static terms.

The patterns of inequality generated from historical precedents and the industrial and occupational mix of high-tech centers closely follow patterns of other industrial sectors in terms of earnings. Where the high-tech sector diverges from other sectors is in terms of earnings profiles and inequality. Regions and local areas that have historically paid lower or higher wages do so in high-tech industries as well. Higher average high-tech wages, however, generate a two-tier earnings profile pattern in most regions. Regional differences in earnings and earnings distributions reflect regional variations in industrial and occupational mix, as demonstrated in chapter 4.

Labor market type affects earnings distributions of high-tech workers in ways that differ from workers in other industrial sectors. Findings based on the national high-tech labor force and high-tech workers in high-tech centers do not always hold for workers in labor markets dominated by other industries. Average earnings are lower among high-tech workers, and earnings inequality is greater among high-tech workers in certain labor market contexts. The socioeconomic outcomes of high-tech industrialization are not uniform in all locales. This is an important point for industrial developers to note.

The most disquieting pattern that characterizes high-tech industry earnings inequality nationally and across all regions and market types pertains to the consequences of minority status. Much more so than for non–high-tech workers, minority labor force status contributes to total earnings inequality among high-tech workers. While we can report some reduction over time in inequality due to the social division of labor, we must also caution that the domestic production jobs that generated this inequality are also in decline. Moreover, occupational divisions with increasing importance for overall high-tech earnings inequality are frequently segregated along gender, race, and ethnic lines. The distinctive occupational configurations of high-tech manufacturing industries and requirements for a flexible labor force create a disadvantageous position for minorities in high-tech industries. Minority workers tend to have little bargaining power and little opportunity for mobility. They are compelled to take any available local employment. High-tech firms have been known to locate production facilities in areas that have an available minority (especially female) labor force. Coupled with an intense aversion to unionization on the part of many high-tech employers, the economic opportunity structure for minority production workers in high-tech industries can only be described as bleak.

In general, the patterns of inequality demonstrated in these analyses conform to a new pattern of inequality that some argue is emerging for the nation as a whole. While increasing opportunities exist for the most highly skilled in the U.S. labor force, the fastest growing job categories are at the bottom of the skill hierarchy. While the expanding service sector needs some highly educated professionals, it needs many more cashiers, waitresses, bartenders, and clerks. Such a transformation of the occupational structure can only lead to polarization of earnings. With the decline of traditional key industries that provide high-skill blue-collar jobs, opportunities for advancement, union wages, and job security, the shrinking of an industrial middle class is inevitable. To this scenario we add the rise of a new industrial sector that, like the services, embodies polarization and inequality within its various divisions of labor.

High-tech industries offer enhanced economic opportunities for many highly skilled, technically trained workers whose salaries tend to raise average earnings for these industries as a whole. At the same time, many high-tech workers are production workers (operators, assemblers, transporters, handlers, and laborers) whose skill requirements and wages are low, whose jobs are quite vulnerable, and who often occupy minority statuses that further diminish their bargaining power in the workplace. One segment of the labor force, located in particular regions and local labor market areas, will undoubtedly experience enhanced economic opportunities through high-tech industrialization. Yet, for many facing already limited opportunity structures, high-tech industrialization will do little to alleviate their economic disadvantage or enhance prospects for mobility.

Chapter Six

High Technology: Fast Lane to the Future or the Past?

Our depiction of the realities of employment, organization, earnings, and inequality in high-technology industries suggests many contradictions. The high-tech sector contains some of the fastest growing components of the U.S. economy but still accounts for less than 10 percent of all U.S. employment. High-tech industries produce sophisticated products that test the limits of our imagination but do so with production processes that frequently consist of simple, tedious manual tasks. In high-tech firms, well-paid, challenging upper-tier jobs with extensive mobility opportunities exist alongside low-wage, insecure, lower-tier positions that have few avenues for advancement. Within single high-tech enterprises, opportunities for participation, responsibility, and autonomy among professional workers contrast sharply with strict discipline, intense supervision, and threat of job loss directed at production workers. Most importantly, a sector that is on the cutting edge of technical innovation appears to be in the Dark Ages in its managerial strategies and organization of work.

More often than not, we find U.S. high-tech industries mirroring other industries. As we speculate about the future of fast-lane work in high technology, we find numerous parallels to other work in manufacturing and services. In this concluding chapter, we attempt to sort these similarities and differences and speculate on the future of this sector.

We have described several flexible production strategies employed in the high-tech sector where flexibility is so important for the viability of firms. While high-tech markets are sometimes dominated by a few large oligopolistic firms, most of these markets are very competitive. Under certain circumstances, small producers can com-

131

pete effectively with large corporations in this sector. Frequent discoveries and innovations in products and production techniques result in very short product cycles. Markets change rapidly as new products emerge and new demands are generated. High-tech markets are volatile and react strongly to peaks and troughs in the business cycle. Firms must constantly adjust, adapt, and change; they must be flexible.

Strategies for maintaining the requisite flexible production can be either static or dynamic. Static measures are characterized by sporadic, discrete, and often profound shifts in size and type of labor force, products rendered, plant locations, and production processes. Using managerial models developed in mature industries outside the sector, high-tech managers maintain a static flexibility by geographically shifting production facilities to take advantage of various types of labor, deskilling or automating work to lessen dependencies on particular types of labor, hiring part-time or temporary workers, using easily replaced minority labor that must settle for low-wages and that demands less in benefits or working conditions, and finally, contingency management of different work groups with techniques that serve to segment and divide labor markets.

The dynamic strategy for flexible production involves constant product and production innovation in a continuous process of change. In the dynamic approach, a mental/manual division of labor is not as pronounced because all workers are active participants in the design and implementation of necessary innovations that maintain flexibility and adaptability. Enterprises of this sort are becoming frontrunners in the high-tech marketplace, setting standards to which other organizations may have to adjust and adapt. Japanese firms have been especially successful in incorporating dynamic production. Despite the advantages associated with this approach, it appears that few U.S. firms have sought or attained this kind of dynamic flexibility as a means of coping with the rapidly changing, volatile environments in which they exist.

While the implications of these different production strategies are many, we have focused on the ways in which static approaches to flexible production, so common in the United States, shape divisions of labor. In high-tech industries the deskilling of production, for example, accentuates two very different tiers in the occupational structure (the technical division of labor). The responsibilities for technical advancement are placed solely in the hands of white-collar professionals, creating a very top-heavy technical division of labor that characterizes these industries. The use of women and minority workers almost exclusively for low-skill and low-paying jobs leads to a social division of labor that is more distinct among high-tech industries than among all other industries combined. A clear high-tech spatial division of labor also emerges in which production is separated from design and firm location strategies tend to maximize union avoidance. While not solely determined by managerial approaches, these divisions of labor are certainly shaped and altered by various static and dynamic practices.

Divisions of labor, be they technical, social, or spatial, contribute to socioeconomic inequality that exists within the high-tech sector and between high-tech workers and those in other industries. We have demonstrated that occupational levels and minority labor force status influence earnings inequality to a greater extent in the high-tech sector than in other industrial sectors. We have also presented evidence of differences in the magnitudes and distributions of earnings among high-tech workers in various regions and local labor market types. In all these analyses it is clear that the sources of inequality and the polarization of earnings that characterize the American economy as a whole are reflected and often exacerbated in the high-tech industrial sector.

While we make no claims about developing a comprehensive theory of high-technology work structures and resulting stratification patterns, we do believe we have assembled some useful ideas that provide a starting point for a coherent research agenda on high-tech industrialization. We have attempted to integrate concepts and constructs from disciplines that share a common interest in understanding high-technology: geography, economics, and sociology. We have used these theoretical tools to interpret our empirical findings and those of other researchers. We have relied on national samples of the high-tech labor force to examine social, spatial, industrial, occupational, and economic variations within the high-tech sector. In retrospect, we continue to be impressed by the variations in work structures among high-tech industries and the variety of socioeconomic outcomes produced within this sector. Researchers, policymakers, and economic development practitioners must acknowledge that high tech can mean many things and can lead to different consequences depending on its context and specific form. Moreover, these consequences are often paradoxical; they are positive for some workers and negative for others.

With this theoretical approach and the knowledge of major trends and variations, our inquiry leads us next to studies at the firm level. It is here that the strategies for static and dynamic flexibility are generated and employed. Through case studies of firms we hope to detect direct socioeconomic effects of flexible production on workers.

Poised on the verge of a new century, we are witnessing a wave of global political and economic transformations. Many of these changes will directly affect the environment in which high-tech industries operate. A reduced emphasis on defense, for example, could force many defense contractors to turn their research and development initiatives to other capital and consumer markets. U.S. scientists and engineers will be encouraged to pursue more public-oriented applications of high technology. Meanwhile, even in these most innovative areas of production, new markets and new producers from nations that have long been prohibited from full participation in the global economy will be challenging U.S. firms and industries.

There can be no doubt that high-tech industries are increasingly important in the U.S. economy's struggle for international viability in consumer and capital goods. We see several elements as crucial to a coherent national policy on high-tech industrialization. The production in the high-tech sector of flexible technologies like computers and robotics, for example, can revitalize other manufacturing industries, providing good jobs for workers in which they can learn, grow, and earn a living wage. It is important that high-tech industries be viewed as something more than an expanding high-wage sector. These industries can play a larger role in the economy through linkages and supports to other manufacturing and service industries. High technology alone is not an answer to industrial decline. As a component of an advancing, diversified economy it could be very important in restoring U.S. competitiveness in global markets.

DYNAMIC SCENARIOS

For high-technology industries to provide a genuine boost to the anemic U.S. economy, this sector must begin to engage in meaningful organizational and managerial innovations. It will take more than technological innovation if U.S. high-tech firms are to meet the challenges of the twenty-first century. Though traditional strategies of static flexibility generate some short-run successes, we doubt their ability to sustain economic growth in a way that ensures the long-run viability of U.S. firms in the global marketplace.

Strategies of dynamic flexibility will take on increasing importance in the development of the high-tech sector. Though American companies have not embraced or perhaps even understood this alternative, models that incorporate dynamic flexibility already exist and compelling visions of new alternatives have been articulated.

The New Craft Production

Piore and Sabel focus their attention on the organization of production, warning of the decline in mass production and the advance of a new age of craft production.[1] Here the static approach of Fordism will be superseded by whole production communities that are flexible in their ability to "continually reshape the productive process through the rearrangement of its components." These communities are also flexibly specialized such that "the set of possible arrangements is bounded and the aim of redeployment limited" by the definition of the industry itself.[2] These communities limit entry either formally or informally so that their resources will not be drained. They encourage types of competition that promote innovation but limit competition that might inhibit innovation in the long run (for example, wage competition). It is the community and not the firm that, "organizes research, recruits labor, and guarantees the flow of supplies and credit."[3] The industrial basis of these communities lies in craft production. Mass production with its complex division of labor, specialized production technologies, and the separation of the design from the execution of work is seen as the antithesis of flexible specialization. The small, high-tech software firm epitomizes the reemergence of craft production as described by Piore and Sabel.

As we have demonstrated, however, a majority of high-tech workers are employed in large-scale mass production. Though the Piore and Sabel model may fit some high-tech workers in craftlike production well, we believe that dynamic flexibility does not have to be limited to small batch or craft production. There is much potential for a dynamic approach to mass production operations. As critics note, few firms or industries adhere completely to true mass production criteria which include high levels of dedicated equipment, little product differentiation, and long production runs.[4] Though it is at the core of Fordism, even the auto industry does not necessarily fit the ideal model of mass production. In fact, it is precisely the auto industry into which Japanese manufacturers have incorporated elements of dynamic flexibility resulting in highly profitable, just-in-time production systems.

Qualitative Growth

In a macroeconomic argument, Fred Block contends that standard neoclassical economic strategies ought to be replaced by a concern for "qualitative growth" as a new postindustrial scenario.[5] By this he means "a highly dynamic economy that is producing progressively higher levels of human satisfaction" in a period of little or no growth, as measured by GNP or some other conventional economic gauge. Dynamically flexible production is a key element of qualitative growth because workers are constantly improving their abilities and firms are continually adapting to upgraded labor forces. Concerns for output focus not so much on commodities as on qualitative dimensions of output. Block lists examples: "work that is intrinsically satisfying, voluntary leisure time, economic security, a safe and clean environment, and a plentitude of community and voluntary services."[6]

Salaried Internal Labor Markets

Paul Osterman takes a different approach, couching his argument in terms of labor market structures.[7] Osterman describes several firms that currently practice the extension of the "salaried" model of internal labor markets to include blue-collar workers. He contrasts this with the traditional "industrial" model that has characterized most mature U.S. industries. Instead of rigid job classifications and wages tightly connected to jobs, a salaried internal labor market is flexibly organized around secure or guaranteed jobs. Flexible production technologies are used by blue-collar workers in broadly defined jobs in which they develop new skills. In essence, these workers forgo the traditional seniority system and its risk of layoffs for increased job security and wages tied to personal criteria—workers' valued skills. Osterman notes that IBM, several new General Motors plants (the Saturn plant in particular), and certain General Electric plants use features of the salaried, internal labor market model. Osterman acknowledges that the security enjoyed by workers in these larger firms often comes at the expense of an increased labor force of part-time, temporary, and outsourced workers who are left to take the bumps and grinds of market fluctuations and uncertainties. This translates into a form of dynamic flexibility for some parts of the firm and static flexibility for others. This is very similar to Japanese firms that offer lifetime employment for some while suppliers and contractors are at the mercy of an ever-changing market.

But Osterman argues that this model in which workers central to the firm fare well while workers on the margins get short shrift has limited potential for the long run. The eventual shortage of flexible labor (minorities, women, and new entrants into the labor force) coupled with perceived problems of commitment and quality rightly or wrongly attributed to this labor force segment may reduce the feasibility of this method of dividing workers. Since employers are wary of the job security aspect of the salaried model, Osterman calls for a public employment policy that promotes job security through measures external to the firm. Policies could include incentives for firms to provide more general training for workers and retraining for displaced workers so they can fill labor shortages within their companies. Still other measures include community training and placement services aimed at mainstream workers but not excluding marginal workers, consortia of small firms that sponsor training programs and draw from a common labor pool as demand warrants, and inducements to companies to prevent layoffs by substituting part-time work for full-time with the provision of unemployment insurance for lost work time.

Workplace Democracy

Salaried internal labor markets could provide a work structure conducive to the use of flexible technologies and continuous innovation and improvement that are vital to dynamic flexibility. Osterman admits, however, that the widespread adoption of the salaried model is contingent either on management changing "in fundamental ways in how it manages its business" or a profound restructuring of the firm.[8] In our minds this must include a fundamental reorganization of employment that leads to genuine workplace democracy. Fred Block argues that it is possible to restructure work so that increasing workers' human capital through dynamic flexibility will result in productivity enhancements. Institutional arrangements are needed that "sustain employees' motivation, encourage them to be heard, and assure high levels of investment in the development of their skill."[9] Workers cannot be expected to learn new skills, create new ways to improve production and products, and commit to firm goals without a much stronger voice in the decisions that affect them and their jobs. In line with this argument, Bennett Harrison and Barry Bluestone write:

> Corporate management alone does not hold the secret of how to produce high-quality, competitive products. It must increasingly rely on the entire range of employees within the firm to develop new techniques of production, judge the applicability and usefulness of new technology, assure quality control, and forge new labor-management relations that enhance productivity and equity within the firm.
> To do all of this, workers and their representatives need to

possess much more information about their industries and the
decision-making process within their firms. They must ultimately share in decisions, not just about wages and working conditions, but about the entire panoply of functions that management has traditionally controlled.... It encompasses control over
the introduction of new technology, decisions about new investments and locations of plants, subcontracting, the design of new
products, and even the pricing of products. Today, perhaps more
than ever, the decisions that management makes unilaterally
about the design, quality, and price of products affect the job
security of workers and the nation's standard of living substantially more than contractual language governing wages, vaca-
tion time, job classifications, and the like. Yet, workers have yet
to share sufficient control over these business matters.[10]

The enhanced level of commitment and participation demanded
of workers in dynamic production must be coupled with a sharing of
control over the firms by workers and management. We agree with
Block that there is much more to workplace democracy than trendy
Quality Circles and worker-employer discussion groups. It is also
likely that sharing control between managers and workers must take
place in a context of shared ownership. But to borrow Block's concept,
whether they are stockholders or "stakeholders," it is imperative that
workers be involved in strategic decision-making. As we have
argued, new technologies and strategies for organizing work can
result in statically or dynamically flexible production. The decisions
governing the use of these technologies are pivotal for the nature of
work, divisions of labor, and inequality in the workplace. Given U. S.
employers' track record in these matters, participation in such decisions by workers seems the best way to ensure that humane and
viable decisions are made.

Though they are only part of a U.S. industrial restructuring,
high-tech industries do have the potential to regenerate other manufacturing and service industries. By providing the technologies for
flexible production, the high-tech sector is a key to revitalization in
other sectors. High-tech industries can also be models of dynamic
flexibility through their own use of these technologies in innovative
work organizations.

The diffusion of new technologies and new ways of organizing
work is often slow. Unions, managers, and workers are often hesitant
to adopt new ways—afraid of losing hard-won gains or taking risks
that might not pay off. To encourage this transformation, fundamen-

tal institutional arrangements will have to be altered. A coherent industrial policy that promotes the development of the high-tech sector as a part of a larger manufacturing and service economy is long overdue. Moreover, employment policies are needed that soften the demands of change for workers and employers alike when new technologies and different divisions of labor are warranted. The inevitable inequalities that follow the unevenness of structural change can be ameliorated by such policies. But there must be a broad-based commitment on the part of workers and employers who must make the changes work. Likewise, policymakers must structure institutional arrangements in feasible ways, and the public must share in the financing of these institutional revisions. Other nations—Japan, Sweden, and West Germany—have met with some success in such ventures, but each of these countries has a very different history, culture, and set of ideologies. Thus, the United States is at a crossroads. Decisions must be made on policies that will affect not only the structures of work and productivity, but equality, equity, and social justice in the American workplace.

WHAT LIES AHEAD?

There is reason for optimism found in the works of Osterman, Block, and Piore and Sabel. Piore and Sabel argue that mass production is on the wane because rising standards of living create demand for more specialized products. This will increasingly force companies into flexible specialization to remain competitive. Block contends that qualitative growth is a feasible and desirable alternative given the trends already underway involving markets, labor, capital, and GNP in postindustrial America.

Osterman notes that some firms are attempting to provide greater employment security to workers and that this issue has become central in collective bargaining. He is optimistic that recent policy initiatives that offer job training for welfare recipients reflect public interest in the right issues—jobs, training, and security. Of course, the focus of such initiatives could be much broader. And, if all else fails, Osterman argues that changing labor force demographics will increase the pool of the least flexible, experienced workers relative to more flexible, secondary laborers. This in turn will force restructuring to address the escalating needs of inflexible workers for security.

Though Block's focus on dynamic flexibility is most similar to our emphasis, the other ideas noted above have clear parallels. Piore and Sable's flexible specialization can be interpreted as a form of dynamic flexibility. Osterman's salaried internal labor markets can be viewed as a commensurate model for the social organization of work implied by dynamic flexibility. Yet, with respect to high tech, we are not as optimistic as the prognosticators we have reviewed here. We have strong reservations about the willingness to change among employers, workers, policymakers, or the public at large. There remain ample signs that the U.S. high-tech sector is bound to a legacy of traditions and conventions that often mirror the declining manufacturing sector.

At a time when the U.S. war economy is winding down, there continue to be those who insist that defense-related research and development are critical.[11] This does not bode well for the transfer of scientific, engineering, and technical expertise to public and consumer-oriented manufacturing problems. The number of students in technical and scientific disciplines continues to be well behind projected demands. Occupational segregation in high tech is compounded because fewer minorities are entering colleges and universities.[12] Computer technology that expands the range of production worker skills in smaller companies is still more likely to deskill workers and centralize management control over them in larger firms.[13] Finally, high-tech industries continue to exhibit traditional flexibility strategies such as capital mobility, deskilling, segmentation of labor markets along racial, ethnic and gender lines, technical and spatial polarization of workers, and contingency management.

Moreover, the firms that are on the cutting edge of technology still lag behind in human resource management. Of course, autonomous work teams and Quality Circles allowing worker input and creativity are increasingly used in many firms. But, as Block argues, the notion of worker participation and the stronger concept of industrial democracy have taken on a hollow ring in many American companies today, and the high-tech sector is no exception. These corporatist strategies too often result in little or no enhancement of workers' ability to influence key decisions.[14] And, while some experiments of this sort have produced positive results, the greatest irony is that most successful experiments are likely to be terminated and replaced by traditional decision-making structures. Erosion of control is not well received by managers even if company costs are reduced and benefits expanded.[15]

Corporatist strategies such as worker participation and quality of worklife projects rest on unrealistic assumptions about the American firm—that it is a unitary, apolitical organization in which all labor is in harmony to achieve a single goal. Academicians from Durkheim to Drucker have espoused this view, but unfortunately they confused this ideal with reality.[16] The real American firm is locked in a stronghold of mistrust and antagonism that has permeated the relationship between labor and management throughout its history. In this volatile context, the introduction of computer technologies that increase flexibility has typically been accompanied by increased rationalization of work,[17] reductions in numbers of workers,[18] and increasingly centralized control of workers with these incredibly thorough instruments of monitoring.[19]

In his praise of the computerization of the New York City government, Thomas Stanback reports a "clear shift from lower-skilled, lower-paid to higher-skilled, higher-paid employment."[20] Yet, this was accompanied by major reductions in lower-level clerical, administrative, and service workers and by increases in higher-level administrators and officials. His enthusiasm for this organizational skill upgrading must be tempered by the fact that those who lost their jobs were not likely to have been those who moved into new managerial slots. Stanback takes heart that "because of a standing policy, no one has lost his or her job. Adjustments are made by reassignment and, in time, by attrition."[21]

Barbara Garson also recounts the computerization of public and private service jobs.[22] In *The Electronic Sweatshop,* she describes the use of computers for the rationalization of work and, moreover, for the centralization and control of workers in a wide range of tasks from taking fast-food orders, to making airline reservations, to social work and even stock brokerage. From the worker's point of view, the rationalization is a mixed blessing. On the one hand, job tasks are often simpler. On the other hand, reorganized jobs become repetitive, less creative, and sometimes more boring. And, the attrition that Stanback anticipates does indeed occur. Garson argues that attrition accelerates as workers quit rather than watch their jobs degenerate into robotlike and thoughtless tasks.

Furthermore, the use of computers has meant a tremendous increase in the capacity to moniter workers. Keystrokes and pages typed have become measures of productivity and serve as criteria for employee evaluation.[23] Both Stanback and Garson note the difficulty in getting middle managers, in particular, to accept the use of computer technologies in their work. Clearly their resistence is not simply the fear of something new but fear of losing security.

Thus, the use of potentially dynamic production technologies like computers and robotics has followed the patterns of specialized, mass production technology found in traditional industries. Too often flexible production is a means to increase efficiency, productivity, and control of organizations, at the expense of meaningful work and workers' jobs. It appears that the social relations of work that have created this legacy will continue to be a barrier to the effective implementation of dynamic flexibility in the American high-tech workplace and beyond. Until these social relations can be fundamentally altered, the use of technology and the delegation of control to create dynamic flexibility will meet with little success.

The adoption of dynamic flexibility in the high-tech sector could assist in the revitalization of the U.S. economy and labor force in ways far beyond increased productivity, personal earnings, and corporate profits. It could mean a more humane and enriching work experience for workers in goods-producing and service-producing sectors of the economy. Yet, like their counterparts in other industries, high-tech employers do not appear to be choosing this approach. In the long run, to compete with Japan and Germany—to stay in the global fast lane—it may be essential that U.S. high-tech firms embrace a dynamically flexible social organization of production. Static flexibility has no place on the cutting edge.

Notes

CHAPTER 1. WORK IN THE FAST LANE: FLEXIBILITY, DIVISIONS OF LABOR, AND INEQUALITY IN HIGH-TECH INDUSTRIES

1. See Katherine Bradbury, "The Shrinking Middle Class" *New England Economic Review* Sept./Oct. (1986): 41–55; Lester Thurow, "The Disappearance of the Middle Class" *New York Times* (Feb. 5, 1984); Bruce Steinberg, "The Mass Market is Splitting Apart" *Fortune* (Nov. 28, 1983): 76–82; Bennett Harrison, Chris Tilly, and Barry Bluestone, "Rising Inequality," in David Obey and Paul Sarbanes, *The Changing American Economy* (New York: Basil Blackwell, 1988): pp. 111–127; Paul Blumberg, *Inequality in an Age of Decline* (New York: Oxford, 1980); McKinley L. Blackburn and David E. Bloom, "What's happening to the Middle Class?" *American Demographics* 7(1986): 19–25; Chris Tilly "U-Turn on Equality: The Puzzle of Middle Class Decline" *Dollars and Sense* 116(1986): 11–13.

2. While Braverman's *Labor and Monopoly Capital: The Degradation of Work in the Twentieth Century* (New York: Monthly Review Press, 1975) was an early initiator of the "deskilling thesis," more recent works such as Barbara Garson's *The Electronic Sweatshop* (New York: Penguin Books, 1988); M. Wallace and A. Kalleburg's "Industrial Transformation and the Decline of Craft: The Decomposition of Skill in the Printing Industry, 1931–1982," *American Sociological Review* 47:307–324; and D. Cornfield, P. A. Phipps, D. P. Bates, D. K. Carter, T. W. Coker, K. E. Kitzmiller, and P. B. Wood's "Office Automation Clerical Workers and Labor Relations in the Insurance Industry," in D. B. Cornfield's *Workers, Manager, and Technological Change: Emerging Patterns of Labor Relations* (New York: Plenum, 1987), pp. 111–134, describe the current deskilling process in various occupations and industries.

3. Parts of this section are taken from our previously published work: Glenna Colclough and Charles Tolbert, "High Technology, Work and Inequality in Southern Labor Markets" *Work and Occupations*, vol. 17, No. 1, pp. 3–29, copyright 1990, by Sage Publications. Reprinted by permission of Sage Publications, Inc.

4. Eva Galambos, "Technician Manpower in the South: High Tech Industries or High Tech Occupations?" Report of the Southern Regional Education Board

(1983), pp. 1–24. To obtain, write Southern Regional Education Board, 1340 Spring Street, N.W., Atlanta, Ga. 30309.

5. For example, Randy Hodson provides some very useful insights for those engaging in research on high-technology industries and firms in his article, "Working in 'High-tech': Researchers and Opportunities for the Industrial Sociologist" in *The Sociological Quarterly*, 26:351–364. However, he assumes that these industries and firms all engage in "high-tech" production processes using computers, robots, etc., which may not always be the case.

6. Richard Riche, Daniel Hecker, and John Burgan, "High Technology Today and Tomorrow: A Small Slice of the Employment Pie" *Monthly Labor Review* (Nov. 1983): 50–58.

7. Edward Malecki, "High Technology and Local Economic Development" *American Planning Association Journal* 50 (1984): 262–269.

8. Randy Hodson, "Good Jobs and Bad Management: How New Problems Evoke Old Solutions in High-Tech Settings," in George Farkas and Paula England (eds.), *Industries, Firms, and Jobs: Sociological and Economic Approaches* (New York: Plenum Press, 1988), pp.247–279.

9. Edward Malecki, "High Technology and Local Economic Development," cited above.

10. Richard Riche et al., "High Technology Today and Tomorrow," cited above.

11. Edward Malecki, "High Technology and Local Economic Development," cited above.

12. Daniel Bell, *The Coming of Post Industrial Society* (New York: Basic Books, 1973); Gerhard E. Lenski, *Power and Privilege* (New York: McGraw-Hill, 1966).

13. Neal Smith, *Uneven Development: Nature, Capital, and the Production of Space,* (New York: Basil Blackwell, 1984); Ernest Mandel, *Late Capitalism,* (London: New Left Books, 1975).

14. See Randy Hodson, "Working in High-Tech," cited above.

CHAPTER 2. THE NATURE AND ORGANIZATION OF HIGH-TECH INDUSTRIES AND FIRMS

1. Annalee Saxenian, "The Urban Contradictions of Silicon Valley: Regional Growth and the Restructuring of the Semiconductor Industry," in Larry Sawers and William Tabb (eds.), *Sunbelt/Snowbelt: Urban Development and Regional Restructuring* (New York: Oxford University Press, 1984), pp. 163–197.

2. Annalee Saxenian, "The Urban Contradictions of Silicon Valley," cited above (p.187).

3. Bennett Harrison, "Regional Restructuring and 'Good Business Climates': The Economic Transformation of New England since World War II," in Larry Sawers and William Tabb (eds.), *Sunbelt/Snowbelt: Urban Development and Regional Restructuring* (New York: Oxford University Press, 1984), pp. 48–96.

4. Ron Wolf, "High-Tech Guru Calls IBM Slow-moving, Vulnerable," in *Huntsville Times* (March 19, 1989), p. 5C. Regis McKenna's book, *Who's Afraid of Big Blue? How Companies Are Challenging IBM and Winning* is available from Addison-Wesley Publishers, 1989.

5. Nancy Dorfman, *Innovation and Market Structure: Lessons from the Computer and Semiconductor Industries* (Cambridge: Ballinger Publishing Co.,1987).

6. Roy Rothwell and Walter Zegveld, *Reindustrialization and Technology* (Armonk, N.Y.: M. C. Sharpe, 1985) argue that some high-tech products have life cycles so short that production can remain at parent plants for all the product cycle. Annalee Saxenian describes the transistor market as an industry that "literally exploded under the steam of ongoing technological innovation.... Within its first twenty years alone, the industry completed the full life cycle for three generations of semiconductory products" (pp. 170 and 192). Annalee Saxenian "The urban contradictions of Silicon Valley," in Sawers and Tabb, *Sunbelt/Snowbelt: Urban Development and Regional Restructuring,* (New York: Oxford University Press, 1984); and Wilson, Ashton, and Egan argue that innovation in the semiconductor industry is so rapid that each new innovation starts a new product cycle in *Innovation, Competition, and Government Policy in the Semiconductor Industry,* (Lexington, Mass.: Lexington Books, 1980), p. 104.

7. Marc Weiss in "High-Technology Industries and the Future of Employment" *Built Environment* 9 (1983): 51–60, discusses the patterns of merger, consolidation, and business failure that have rapidly led to concentration in the electronics industry, for example.

8. Stephen Cohen and John Zysman, *Manufacturing Matters: The Myth of the Post-Industrial Economy* (New York: Basic Books, 1987).

9. Ibid., p. 131

10. Fred Block. *Postindustrial Possibilities: A Critique of Economic Discourse* (Berkeley: University of California Press, 1990), p. 195.

11. Stephen Cohen and John Zysman, *Manufacturing Matters,* cited above, p. 132.

12. John Alic and Martha Caldwell Harris, "Employment Lessons from the U.S. Electronics Industry," in R. E. Pahl (ed.), *On Work: Historical, Comparative and Theoretical Approaches* (New York: Basil Blackwell, 1988), pp. 670–683.

13. Ibid., pp. 678–679.

14. Interview conducted by authors with Buddy French, executive vice president of human resources of a multinational computer software and hardware manufacturing firm, Intergraph.

15. Edward Malecki, "High Technology and Local Economic Development" *American Planning Association Journal* 5 (1984): 262–269.

16. See, for example, John Keller, "The Division of Labor in Electronics," in June Nash and Maria Patricia Fernandez-Kelly (eds.), *Women, Men, and the International Division of Labor* (New York: State University of New York Press, 1983), pp. 346–373; and Marc Weiss, "High Technology Industries and the Future of Employment" *Built Environment* 9(1983): 51–60.

17. See Peter Doeringer and Michael J. Piore, *Internal Labor Markets and Manpower Analysis* (Lexington, Mass.: D. C. Heath, 1971) for a description of primary and secondary labor markets.

18. Robert Snow, "The New International Division of Labor and the U.S. Work Force: The Case of the Electronics Industry," in June Nash and Maria Patricia Fernandez-Kelly (eds.), *Women, Men, and the International Division of Labor* (New York: State University of New York Press, 1983), pp. 39–69.

19. Susan S. Green, "Silicon Valley's Women Workers: A Theoretical Analysis of Sex Segregation in the Electronics Industry Labor Market," in June Nash and Maria Patricia Fernandez-Kelly (eds.), *Women, Men, and the International Division of Labor* (New York: State University of New York Press, 1983), pp. 273–331.

20. Naomi Katz and David Kemnitzer, "Fast Forward: The Internationalization of Silicon Valley," in June Nash and Maria Patricia Fernandez-Kelly (eds.), *Women, Men, and the International Division of Labor* (New York: State University of New York Press, 1983), pp. 332–345.

21. Ibid.

22. Interview conducted by authors with the chief executive officer of a diversified, high-tech manufacturing firm. Due to the sensitive nature of this person's comments, the person asked not to be identified.

23. Susan Green, "Silicon Valley's Women Workers: A Theoretical Analysis of Sex Segregation in the Electronics Industry Labor Market" cited above.

24. Ibid., p. 292.

25. Interview conducted by authors with a plant manager at a branch of a major high-tech manufacturing firm. This person asked to not be identified.

26. "High-Tech Industry Not the Answer For All Rural Areas," [Based on an interview with James Miller of Economic Research Service (USDA)] *Farmline* 9 (1988): 8–9.

27. Eva Galambos, "Technician Manpower in the South: High-Tech Industries or High Tech Occupations?" Report of the Southern Regional Education Board (1983):1–24.

28. Liz Atwood, "Women Engineers: Few females will choose profession despite opportunities, pay" reported in *The Huntsville Times* (Nov. 26, 1989) p. 2F.

29. John Keller, "The Division of Labor in Electronics," cited above.

30. Evelyn Glenn and Charles M. Tolbert, "Technology and Emerging Patterns of Stratification for Women of Color: Race and Gender Segregation in Computer Occupations," in Barbara D. Wright (ed.), *Women, Work, and Technology* (Ann Arbor: University of Michigan Press, 1987), pp. 318–331.

31. Linda Brewster Stearns and Charlotte Colemen, "Occupational Segregation by Sex in High- and Low-Technology Manufacturing Industries," in Ida Simpson and Richard Simpson (eds.), *Research in the Sociology of Work*, vol. 4 (Greenwich, Conn.: JAI Press, 1988), pp. 289–310.

32. John Keller, "The Division of Labor in Electronics," cited above.

33. Ibid., p. 367.

34. David T. Cook, "High Tech Versus U.S. Labor Unions" *Christian Science Monitor*, (Sept. 9, 1983), p. 1.

35. Interview conducted by authors with the chief executive officer of a major high-tech manufacturing firm, cited above.

36. Gregg Robinson and Judith McIlwee, "Obstacles to Unionization in High-Tech Industries" *Work and Occupations* 16 (1989): 115–136.

37. Randy Hodson, "Good Jobs and Bad Management: How New Problems Evoke Old Solutions in High-Tech Settings," in George Farkas and Paula England (eds.), *Industries, Firms and Jobs: Sociological and Economic Approaches* (New York: Plenum Press, 1988), pp. 247–279.

38. Naomi Katz and David Kemnitzer, "Fast Forward: The Internationalization of Silicon Valley," cited above.

39. Manuel Castells and Alejandro Portes, "World Underneath: The Origins, Dynamics, and Effects of the 'Informal Economy'," presented at the Conference on Comparative Study of the Informal Sector, Harpers Ferry, West Virginia, 1986.

40. Naomi Katz and David Kemnitzer, "Fast Forward: The Internationalization of Silicon Valley," p. 343.

41. See Doeringer and Piore, cited above, for a definitive discussion of internal labor markets.

42. See Thierry Noyelle, *Beyond Industrial Dualism* (Boulder, Colo.: Westview, 1987); and Paul Osterman *Employment Futures* (New York: Oxford University Press, 1988).

43. Arthur Stinchcombe and Carol Heimer, "Interorganizational Relations and Careers in Computer Software Firms," in Ida Simpson and Richard Simpson (eds.), *Research in the Sociology of Work*, vol. 4 (Greenwich, Conn.: JAI Press, 1988), pp. 179–204.

44. Ibid., p. 180.

45. Ibid., p. 200.

46. See, for example, Randy Hodson, "Good Jobs and Bad Management: How New Problems Evoke Old Solutions," cited above, and Susan Green, "Silicon Valley's Women Workers.

47. Interview by authors with the chief executive officer of a major high-tech manufacturing firm, cited above.

48. See, for example, Michael Eisenscher, *Silicon Valley: A Digest of Electronics Data,* (San Jose, Calif., 1984) and Russell Rumberger and Harry Levin, "The Educational Implications of High Technology" Project Report No. 83–A4, Institute for Research on Educational finance and governance, Stanford University, both cited in Randy Hodson's, "Good Jobs and Bad Management," cited above.

49. John Keller, "The Division of Labor in Electronics," cited above.

50. Fred Block, *Postindustrial Possibilities,* cited above, pp. 96–103.

51. See, for example, Paul Adler, "Tools for Resistance: Workers Can Make Automation Their Ally," *Dollars and Sense* 100 (1984): 708; and M. Cross, "Skill Requirements for Process Industries" *Employment Gazette* 91 (1983): 184–187. See also Randy Hodson, "God Jobs and Bad Management," cited above.

52. Ross Koppel, Eileen Appelbaum, and Peter Albin, "Implications of Workplace Information Technology," in Ida Simpson and Richard Simpson (eds.), *Research in the Sociology of Work,* vol. 4, (Greenwich, Conn.: JAI Press, 1988), pp. 125–152.

53. Burton Klein, "Dynamic Competition and Productivity Advances," in Ralph Landau and Nathan Rosenberg (eds.), *The Positive-Sum Strategy: Harnessing Technology for Economic Growth* (Washington, D.C.: National Academy Press, 1986), p.78.

54. Charles Sabel, *Work and Politics: The Division of Labor in Industry* (New York: Cambridge University Press, 1982).

55. Ibid., pp. 201, 210, 223.

56. Martin, James. "RAD Designed to Facilitate Dynamic Change in Firms," *PC Week* 6, No. 50 (Dec. 18, 1989): 64.

57. Paul Lillrank and Noriaki Kano, *Continuous Improvement: Quality Control Circles in Japanese Industries* (Ann Arbor: University of Michigan, 1989).

58. Randy Hodson, "Good Jobs and Bad Management," cited above.

59. Ibid., p. 266.

60. Ibid., pp. 270–271.

61. Robert Kaufman, Toby Parcel, Michael Wallace and William Form,

"Looking Forward: Responses to Organizational and Technological Change in an Ultra-High-Technology Firm," in Ida Simpson and Richard Simpson (eds.), *Research in the Sociology of Work*, vol. 4 (Greenwich, Conn.: JAI Press, 1988), pp. 31–67.

62. Denise Bielby, William Brastow, and William Bielby, "Goal Incongruence, Interdependence, and Decision-Making in a 'High-Tech' Firm," in Ida Simpson and Richard Simpson (eds.), *Research in the Sociology of Work*, vol. 4 (Greenwich, Conn.: JAI Press, 1988), pp. 153–178.

63. Interview by authors with the chief executive officer of a major high-tech manufacturing firm, cited above.

64. See for example, John Witte, *Democracy, Authority, and Alienation in Work: Workers' Participation American Corporation* (Chicago: University of Chicago Press, 1980); Glenna Colclough, *Humanization of Work Programs and Their Outcomes* unpublished masters Thesis, Kent State University, 1976; and Special Task Force to the Secretary of Health, Education and Welfare, *Work in America* (Cambridge, Mass.: MIT Press, 1983).

CHAPTER 3. EMPLOYMENT IN HIGH-TECH INDUSTRIES: TECHNICAL AND SOCIAL DIVISIONS OF LABOR

1. The CPS Annual Demographic Files used here were conducted annually in March from 1971 through 1988. Questions in the March CPS refer to longest job during the previous year and total earnings from that year. Thus, we label our data points on tables and figures as 1970 through 1987 even though the data were collected in March of each subsequent year (1971 to 1988). We begin with the 1971 March CPS file because of changes in the detail of industry codes initiated at that time that permit us to distinguish high-tech industries from other manufacturing industries.

2. See Russell W. Rumberger and Henry M. Levin, "Forecasting the Impact of New Technologies on the Future Job Market." *Technological Forecasting and Social Change* 27 (1985): 399–417; and Richard Riche, Daniel Hecker, and John Burgan, "High Technology Today and Tomorrow: A Small Slice of the Employment Pie," *Monthly Labor Review* (1983): 50–58.

3. By labor force participant, we mean a person 14 years of age or older who reported working for pay at least one week during the year preceding the survey.

4. Following Singelmann, the service sector here is defined very broadly to include medical, legal, and educational services as well as public administration. See Joachim Singelmann, "The Sectoral Transformation of the Labor Force in Seven Industrialized Countries, 1920–1970." *American Journal of Sociology* 83 (1978): 1224–1234.

5. For illustration purposes, several smaller industries are combined with large ones in Figure 3.2: plastics is grouped with drugs and medicines, engines and turbines

with electrical machinery, and photographic equipment and optical and health equipment with scientific instruments.

6. The occupational categories used throughout this book are based on the 1980 Census occupation classification scheme. In Figure 3.3, our other white-collar category includes the Census major occupation categories of sales occupations; administrative support including clerical; and protective services. Our blue-collar category contains the Census categories of private household service; farming, forestry, and fishing; machine operators, assemblers, and inspectors; transportation and material moving occupations; and handlers, equipment cleaners, helpers, and laborers. The 1980 coding scheme was implemented in the March 1983 CPS. Occupational data for prior survey years have been recoded to match the 1980 Census categories using a template we obtained from the Bureau of the Census. For further information, see Nancy F. Rytina and Suzanne M. Bianchi, "Occupational Reclassification and Changes in Distribution by Gender." *Monthly Labor Review* March (1984): 11–17. While the transformation of these codes is not exact, we believe there is very little error introduced by our use of very broad occupation groups.

7. Several items from the shrinking middle-class literature are cited in the first chapter under note 1.

8. Another approach to smoothing the data points would involve decycling the data with an indicator of business activity such as change in some leading indicator. In this descriptive analysis, we believe it best to allow the data to exhibit cyclical influences.

CHAPTER 4. HIGH-TECH INDUSTRIAL DEVELOPMENT AND THE SPATIAL DIVISION OF LABOR

1. Joseph Schumpeter, *Business Cycles* (New York, McGraw-Hill, 1939).

2. Robert Wilson, Peter K. Ashton and Thomas P. Egan, *Innovation, Competition, and Government Policy in the Semiconductor Industry* (Lexington, Mass.: Lexington Books, 1980).

3. Roy Rothwell and Walter Zegveld, *Reindustrialization and Technology* (Armonk, N.Y.: M. E. Sharpe,1985).

4. F. Townsend, F. Henwood, G. Thomas, K. Pavitt, and S. Wyatt, "Innovation in Britain since 1945," Occasional Paper Series, No. 16, Science Policy Research Unit, University of Sussex, cited in Rothwell and Zegveld, *Reindustrialization and Technology.*

5. Richard Riche, Daniel Hecker, and John Burgan, "High Technology Today and Tomorrow: A Small Slice of the Employment Pie," *Monthly Labor Review* (1983): 50–58.

6. Allan Hunt and Timothy Hunt, "Human Resource Implication for

Robotics," W. E. Upjohn Institute for Employment Research, University of Michigan, cited in Randy Hodson and Robert E. Parker, "Work in High-Technology Settings: A Review of the Empirical Literature," in Ida Simpson and Richard Simpson (eds.), *Research in the Sociology of Work,* vol. 4, (Greenwich, Conn.: JAI Press, 1988), pp. 1–29.

7. "The Speedup in Automation," *Business Week* (Aug. 3, 1981), cited in Marc A. Weiss, "High–Technology Industries and the Future of Employment," *Built Environment* 9: 51-60.

8. Eileen Applebaum, "High Tech and the Structural Employment Problems of the 1980's," in Eileen L. Collins and Lucretia Dewey Tanner, *American Jobs and the Changing Industrial Base* (Cambridge, Mass.: Ballinger Publishing Co., 1984), pp. 23–48.

9. Richard Nelson, *High Technology Policies: A Five Nation Comparison* (Washington D.C.: American Enterprise Institute for Public Policy Research, 1984).

10. Bennett Harrison and Barry Bluestone, *The Great U-Turn: Corporate Restructuring and the Polarizing of America* (New York: Basic Books, 1988).

11. Bill Powell, Bradley Martin, and John Barry, "The Rise of the Trade Hawks" *Newsweek* (March 13, 1989), pp. 46–47.

12. Southern Growth Policies Board, "Halfway Home and a Long Way to Go," the Report of the 1989 Commission on the Future of the South. To obtain, write: Southern Growth Policies Board, P.O. Box 12293, Research Triangle Park, N.C. 27709.

13. This information was obtained from Jim Reichardt, the head of the economic development division of the Huntsville, Alabama, Chamber of Commerce, in an interview with the authors.

14. Robert Sklar, "The American Electronics Industry: An Economic Development Perspective" *Economic Development Review* 3 (1985): 61–69.

15. Interview conducted by authors with the head of the economic development division of the Huntsville Chamber of Commerce, cited above.

16. Bennett Harrison and Barry Bluestone, *The Great U-Turn,* cited above.

17. Michael Luger and Harvey Goldstein, "Science/Research Parks as Instruments of Technology-Based Regional Policy: An Assessment," paper presented at North American meetings of the Regional Science Association, Toronto, Canada, Nov. 11–13, 1988.

18. Edward Bee, "Courting High Tech Industry: Not a Quick Marriage for Most Developers," *Economic Development Review* 3 (1985): 7–12.

19. Richard Walker, "Technological Determination and Determinism: Industrial Growth and Location," in Manuel Castells (ed.), *High Technology, Space, and Society* (Beverly Hills: Sage Publications, 1985), pp. 226–264.

20. See Leonard Bloomquist, "Performance of the Rural Manufacturing Sector," in *Economic Development in the 1980's: Preparing for the Future* (Washington, D.C.: ERS, USDA, 1989); and William Falk and Thomas Lyson, *High Tech, Low Tech and No Tech: Industrial and Occupational Change in the South* (Albany, N.Y.: State University of New York Press, 1988), for examples of the use of product cycle theory to explain development patterns of high-tech industries, especially in rural areas.

21. Richard Walker, "Technological Determination and Determinism," cited above.

22. "Manpower-Related Factors Rank Most Important When Choosing Plant Site Locations" *Electronic Business* 15 (May 1983): 22, cited in Robert Sklar, "The American Electronics Industry," cited above.

23. Chris Paul, "The Impact of Commercial High Technology firms on the Madison County and Alabama Economy," Center for High Technology Management and Economic Research, UAH Research Report No. 360, Huntsville, Ala., p. 8. To obtain, write to Chris Paul, Dept. of Economics, School of Administrative Science, University of Alabama in Huntsville, Huntsville, Ala. 35899.

24. Richard Peet, "Relations of Production and the Relocation of United States Manufacturing Industry Since 1960" *Economic Geography* 59 (1983): 112–143.

25. Ibid., p. 128.

26. Neal Smith, *Uneven Development: Nature, Capital, and the Production of Space* (New York: Basil Blackwell, 1984).

27. Ernest Mandel, *Late Capitalism* (London: New Left Books, 1975), cited in Neal Smith, *Uneven Development*, cited above.

28. Neal Smith, *Uneven Development*, p. 129, cited above.

29. Michael Storper and Richard Walker, "The Spatial Division of Labor: Labor and the Location of Industries," in Larry Sawers and William Tabb, *Sunbelt/Snowbelt: Urban Development and Regional Restructuring* (New York: Oxford University Press, 1984), pp. 19–47.

30. Ibid., p. 19.

31. Ibid.

32. Richard Walker, "Technological Determination and Determinism," p. 243, cited above.

33. Michael Storper, "Technology and Spatial Production Relations: Disequilibrium, Interindustry Relationships, and Industrial Development," in Manuel Castells (ed.), *High Technology, Space, and Society*, pp. 265–283, cited above.

34. Ibid., p. 274.

35. See Manuel Castells, "High Technology, Economic Restructuring, and the Urban-Regional Process in the United States," in Manuel Castells, *High Technology, Space, and Society,* cited above; and Neal Smith, *Uneven Development,* cited above.

36. Michael Storper, "Technology and Spatial Production Relations," pp. 268–269, cited above.

37. Amy Glasmeier, "High-Tech Industries and the Regional Division of Labor," *Industrial Relations* 25 (1986): 197–212.

38. Manuel Castells, "High Technology, Economic Restructuring and the Urban-Regional Process in the United States," cited above.

39. See Annalee Saxenian, "The Urban Contradictions of Silicon Valley: Regional Growth and the Restructuring of the Semiconductor Industry," pp. 163–197, and Bennett Harrison, "Regional Restructuring and 'Good Business Climates': The Economic Transformation of New England since World War II," pp. 48–96, both in Larry Sawers and William K. Tabb (eds.), *Sunbelt/Snowbelt,* cited above, for analyses of high-tech development in Silicon Valley and the Boston area, respectively. See Amy Glasmeier, "Innovative Manufacturing Industries" and "High-Tech Industries and the Regional Division of Labor," both cited above, for analyses using the state as the unit of analysis.

40. Robert Snow, "The New International Division of Labor and the U.S. Work Force: The Case of the Electronics Industry," in June Nash and Maria Fernandez-Kelly (eds.), *Women, Men, and the International Division of Labor* (Albany, N.Y.: State University of New York Press, 1983), pp. 39–69.

41. See Charles Tolbert and Molly Killian, *Labor Market Areas for the United States,* (Washington, D.C.:Economic Research Service, USDA, 1987), for an in-depth discussion of the labor market area identification developed for PUMS-D Census data.

42. Amy Glasmeier, Peter Hall, and Ann Markusen, "Recent Evidence on High-Technology Industries' Spatial Tendencies: A Preliminary Investigation," in *Technology, Innovation and Regional Economic Development: Census of State Government Initiatives for High-Technology Industrial Development—Background Paper* (Washington, D.C.: U.S. Congress, Office of Technology Assessment, May 1983), pp. 145–167.

43. This bias is not problematic in that Glasmeier's (1985) study of high-tech industries finds that large production establishments are for the most part responsible for high concentrations of high-tech employment in certain states.

44. Richard Peet, "Relations of Production and the Relocation of United States Manufacturing Industry Since 1960," cited above.

45. Ibid.

46. Gary Green, *Finance Capital and Uneven Development* (Boulder, Colo.: Westview Press, 1987).

47. Ibid., p. 88.

48. Amy Glasmeier, "High-Tech Industries and the Regional Division of Labor," cited above.

49. Ann Markusen and Robin Bloch, "Defensive Cities: Military Spending, High Technology and Human Settlements," in Manuel Castells (ed.), *High Technology, Space, and Society,* pp. 106–120, cited above.

50. See Amy Glasmeier, Peter Hall, and Ann Markusen, "Recent Evidence on High-Technology Industries' Spatial Tendencies"; and Robert Sklar, "The American Electronics Industry," both cited above.

51. See Robert Sklar, "The American Electronics Industry"; Amy Glasmeier, Peter Hall, and Ann Markusen, "Recent Evidence on High-Technology Industries' Spatial Tendencies"; and William Falk and Thomas Lyson, *High Tech, Low Tech, No Tech,* all cited above.

52. William Falk and Thomas Lyson, in *High Tech, Low Tech, No Tech,* p. 45, cited above.

CHAPTER 5. EARNINGS AND INEQUALITY IN HIGH-TECH INDUSTRIES: NATIONAL, REGIONAL, AND LOCAL PATTERNS

1. See for example, Katharine Bradbury, "The Shrinking Middle Class" *New England Economic Review* Sept./Oct. (1986): 41–55; Lester Thurow, "The Disappearance of the Middle Class" *New York Times,* Feb. 5, 1984; Bennett Harrison, Chris Tilly, and Barry Bluestone, "Rising Inequality," in David R. Obey and Paul Sarbanes (eds.), *The Changing American Economy* (New York: Basic Books, 1986), pp. 111–127.

2. While no specific reference is made to high-tech industries, these economic arguments are discussed in George Farkas, Paula England, and Margaret Barton, "Structural Effects on Wages: Sociological and Economic Views," in George Farkas and Paula England (eds.), *Industries, Firms, and Jobs: Sociological and Economic Approaches* (New York: Plenum Press, 1988), pp. 83–112.

3. These are the same CPS data that were used in the third chapter. See the text there for details.

4. Barry Bluestone and Bennett Harrison, *The Deindustrialization of America: Plant Closings, Community Abandonment, and the Dismantling of Basic Industry* (New York: Basic Books, 1982).

5. Eric Hanushek, "Regional Differences in the Structure of Earnings" *Review of Economics and Statistics* 55 (1973): 204–213; Bennett Harrison, *Education, Training and the Urban Ghetto* (Baltimore: Johns Hopkins University Press, 1972); Mark Fossett and Omer R. Galle, "Community Context and the Structure of Earnings Attainment: A Comparative Investigation of Structure and Process in American Metropolitan Communities" Paper No. 2.004, Texas Population Research Center,

University of Texas, Austin, 1980; E. M. Beck and Glenna Colclough, "Schooling and Capitalism: The Effect of Urban Economic Structure on the Value of Education," in George Farkas and Paula England (eds.), *Industries, Firms, and Jobs: Sociological and Economic Approaches* (New York: Plenum Press, 1988), pp. 113–139; Patrick M. Horan and Charles M. Tolbert, *The Organization of Work in Rural and Urban Labor Markets* (Boulder, Colo.: Westview Press, 1984).

6. Leonard Bloomquist and Gene F. Summers, "Organization of Production and Community Income Distribution" *American Sociological Review* 47 (1982): 325–338; Robert Bibb, "The Industrial Composition of Local Labor Markets: Sex Stratification and Intermetropolitan Structure of Blue-Collar Earnings," unpublished paper, Dept. of Sociology and Anthropology, Vanderbilt University, 1982.

7. Michael Betz, "The City as a System Generating Income Inequality" *Social Forces* 51 (1972): 192–198; Mark Fossett and Omer Galle, "Community Context and the Structure of Earnings Attainment," cited above.

8. Toby Parcel, "Race, Regional Labor Markets, and Earnings," *American Sociological Review* 44 (1979): 262–279.

9. Charles Mueller, "City Effects on Socioeconomic Achievements: The Case of Large Cities," *American Sociological Review* 39 (1974): 652–667.

10. E. M. Beck and Glenna Colclough, "Schooling and Capitalism," cited above.

11. See George Farkas, Paula England, and Margaret Barton, "Structural Effects on Wages, Sociological and Economic views," in George Farkas and Paula England (eds.), *Industries, Firms, and Jobs,* pp. 93–112, cited above.

12. James Cobb, "Y'all Come on Down: The Southern States Pursuit of Industry," *Southern Exposure* 14 (1986): 18–23.

13. Readers are cautioned about the small number of workers in service high-tech industries (26) in the sample for the Midwest region.

14. William Falk and Thomas Lyson, *High Tech, Low Tech, No Tech: Recent Industrial and Occupational Change in the South* (Albany, N.Y.: State University of New York Press, 1988).

15. Portions of this section are from an article by the authors, Glenna Colclough and Charles Tolbert, "High Technology, Work and Inequality in Southern Labor Markets" *Work and Occupations,* vol. 17, No. 1, pp. 3–29, copyright 1990 by Sage Publications, Inc.

CHAPTER 6. HIGH TECHNOLOGY:
FAST LANE TO THE FUTURE OR THE PAST?

1. Michael J. Piore and Charles F. Sabel, *The Second Industrial Divide* (New York: Basic Books, 1984).

2. Ibid., p. 269.

3. Ibid., p. 273.

4. See Karel Williams, Tony Cutler, John Williams and Colin Haslam, "The End of Mass Production?" *Economy and Society* 16 (1987): 405–438.

5. Fred Block, *Postindustrial Possibilities: A Critique of Economic Discourse* (Berkeley: University of California Press, 1990).

6. Ibid., pp. 196–197.

7. Paul Osterman, *Employment Futures: Reorganization, Dislocation, and Public Policy* (New York: Oxford University Press, 1988).

8. Ibid., p. 148.

9. See Block, *Postinduatrial Possibilities*, p. 199, cited above.

10. Bennett Harrison and Barry Bluestone, in *The Great U-Turn: Corporate Restructuring and the Polarizing of America* (New York: Basic Books, 1984), p. 185.

11. Speech by Major General John Peppers, Deputy Commanding General, United States of America Strategic Defense Command, at Technology and Business Symposia (Huntsville, Alabama: May 16, 1990).

12. Simson L. Garfinkel, "More Scientists, Engineers Needed for Increasingly Technical U.S." *Huntsville Times,* (June 15, 1990): p. B1.

13. Maryellen Kelley, "New Process Technology, Job Design, and Work Organization," *American Sociological Review* 55 (1990): 191–208.

14. See Cohen and Zysman, *Manufacturing Matters: The Myth of the Post-Industrial Economy* (New York: Basic Books, 1987), p. 209, for a further description of the concept "corporatism."

15. Alecia Swasy and Carol Hymonitz, "The Workplace Revolution," *Wall Street Journal* (Feb. 9, 1990): p. R8.

16. See Stephen P. Waring, *Taylorism Transformed: Scientific Management Theory* (Chapel Hill, N.C.: University of North Carolina Press, 1991) for an insightful discussion of the roots of contemporary corporatist ideology.

17. See Thomas Stanback, *Computerization and the Transformation of Employment* (Boulder, Colo.: Westview Press, 1987).

18. Both Paul Osterman in *Employment Futures* and Thomas Stanback in *Computerization and the Transformation of Employment,* both cited above, make this point.

19. See Barbara Garson, *The Electronic Sweatshop* (New York: Penguin Books, 1989); and Robert Howard, "Brave New Workplace," reprinted in D. Stanley Eitzen and Maxine Baca Zinn (eds.), *The Reshaping of America: Social Consequences of the Changing Economy* (Englewood Cliffs, N.J.: Prentice-Hall, 1989), pp. 47–57.

20. See Thomas Stanback, *Computerization and the Transformation of Employment*, p. 33, cited above.

21. Ibid., p. 28.

22. See Barbara Garson, *The Electronic Sweatshop*, cited above.

23. Ibid., p. 180.

Index